Countryside Walks in

WESSEX

Edited by Steve Parker

Photography by Michael Busselle

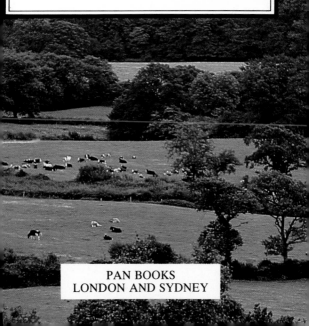

PAN BOOKS
LONDON AND SYDNEY

Contents

First published 1985 by
Travellers Press,
59 Grosvenor Street
London W1X 9DA

This edition published 1988 by
Pan Books Limited,
Cavaye Place,
London SW10 9PG

9 8 7 6 5 4 3 2 1

© Hennerwood Publications 1985

ISBN 0 330 30392 9

Printed in Hong Kong

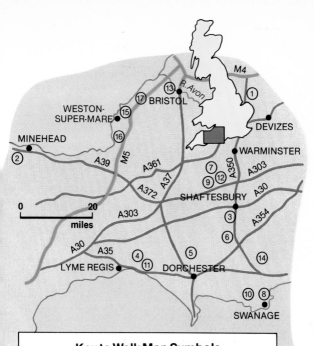

Key to Walk Map Symbols

y/m/a/f	Yards, miles, acres, feet	++++++	Railway
✳	Starting point	≈	River or canal
P	Parking/car park	～	Minor river/stream
i	Information office	====	Waterfall
T	Toilets	≍	Bridge
✕	Picnic site		Sea or lake
◉	Viewpoint		Sand or beach
⌁	Seat	🌿🌿🌿	Woodland
⟶	Direction of route	●	Individual tree
⇰	Alternative routes	ѵѵѵ	Heathland
-----	Route for walkers		Parkland or green
—	Route for disabled	▲▲▲	Rocks
▬	Motorway	○	Cave
—	All other roads	●	Pen pit
➡	One-way traffic	ѵѵѵ	Marsh or bog
----	Ancient way	○	Well
---	Long-distance path	■	Building
-----	Footpath or track	†	Church or chapel
⟫⟫⟫	Steep descent/ascent	✕	Cross
⊔⊔⊔⊔	Steps	∧	Tumulus/stdg stones
▲	Dangerous path	▲	Memorial
∞∞∞	Wall	△	Youth hostel
⚡·	Electric fence	▲	Trigonometric point

Walk Selector

Number	Name	☐ Easy ☐ Moderate ■ Difficult	Length (miles)	Time (hours)
1*	Lacock		$2\frac{1}{2}$	$1\frac{1}{2}$
2	Selworthy		3	2
3	Fontmell Down		4	2
4	Lambert's Hill Forts		$4\frac{1}{2}$	$2\frac{1}{2}$
5*	Cerne Giant		$4\frac{1}{2}$	$2\frac{1}{2}$
6	Ringmoor & Turnworth		5	$2\frac{1}{2}$
7	Gasper Mill		5	$2\frac{1}{2}$
8	Studland		6	3
9*	Stourhead		$6\frac{1}{4}$	3
10	Corfe & Grange Arch		$6\frac{1}{2}$	$3\frac{1}{2}$
11	Golden Cap		$7\frac{1}{2}$	4
12	White Sheet Hill		$7\frac{1}{2}$	4
13	Leigh Woods & Avon		9	$4\frac{1}{2}$
14	Badbury & Kingston		$9\frac{1}{2}$	5
15	Weston & Sand Bay		10	5
16	Brean Down		10	5
17	Clevedon & Cadbury		11	6

★ Facilities for disabled people. Fees payable at most car parks (NT parking free for NT members)

Start/finish P Car park	Grid ref	OS map 1:50,000	OS map 1:25,000
Lacock Abbey P	ST 917 683	173	ST 86/96
Selworthy village P	SS 920 467	181	SS 84/94
Fontmell Magna (roadside)	ST 865 169	183/184	ST 81/91
Lambert's, Coney's, Pilsdon P	SY 366 988 SY 372 977 ST 415 009	193 193 193	SY 29/39 SY 29/39 ST 40/50
Cerne Abbas (roadside)	ST 666 011	194	ST 60/70
Okeford Hill P	ST 812 093	194	ST 80/90
Stourhead P	ST 779 340	183	ST 63/73
Bankes Arms P	SZ 037 825	195	SY 87/97
Stourhead P	ST 779 340	183	ST 63/73
Corfe village P	SY 959 819	195	ST 87/97
Langdon Hill P	SY 412 932	193	SY 49/59
Stourhead P	ST 779 340	183	ST 63/73
Clifton Suspension Bridge, Bristol side P	ST 567 732	172	ST 47/57
Badbury Rings P	ST 961 032	195	ST 80/90
Birnbeck Pier P	ST 329 633	182	ST 26/36
Ford Common (trackside)	ST 303 538	182	ST 25/35
All Saints Lane, Clevedon (roadside)	ST 417 718	172	ST 47/57

Introduction

Much of the land covered by the walks in this book belongs to The National Trust for Places of Historic Interest or Natural Beauty. The NT has twin aims: to provide access to its land and buildings where possible, but at the same time to conserve the landscape, its wildlife and its architecture. This means striking a balance between utilization and preservation. Walkers can play their part by following the country code, and of course by supporting the NT.

The rambles have been devised with novice walkers and family outings in mind. But being a novice does not imply being careless or thoughtless. You need to plan your day in advance. First read the walk account and become familiar with the route on good maps. Next, check ahead on opening times and work out a rough schedule of walking, visits, rest and refreshments. Equip yourself with the right kind of clothing and supplies. Out on the ramble, keep your wits about you: field boundaries may have been moved, trees taken away or new roads constructed.

To give you some idea of what to expect, the walks

have been graded. EASY walks take around two hours and are generally well signposted along made-up paths and tracks. MODERATE walks take up to four hours or so; the terrain is mostly firm but there may be an occasional steep climb or rough track. DIFFICULT walks need careful planning, take the best part of a day, and demand detailed maps, compass, refreshments and suitable clothing.

Walking in the Wessex region – Somerset, Avon, Wiltshire, Dorset and Hampshire – is particularly rewarding if you delve into history. Pre-Roman hill forts, ancient connections with King Arthur and other legendary figures, the medieval barns and field systems, and many other aspects combine to delight historians of all persuasions. For the naturalist there are open chalk downs, miles of hedgerows, and forgotten woodlands. Other routes take the rambler along coastal paths over the cliffs of the Dorset coast through to the Nature Reserve adjacent to Poole harbour or, for instance, inland to the headquarters of the Wessex region, Stourhead, where there is a selection of three fine walks of varying lengths and fascination bordering on Thomas Hardy's countryside. Whatever your interests there is a walk for you – so put one foot in front of the other, and repeat as necessary!

◁ *Cows graze near the Gordano Valley, west of Bristol. Walkers should respect the needs of all country-dwellers*

△ *Heather and gorse bloom on the Studland peninsula, Dorset, turning the rolling heaths to royal purple in the late summer and autumn*

Countryside Care

The countryside lives and breathes. It is home for many, provides a living for some, and plays a vital role in our economy. It is also the basis of our natural heritage.

Those who walk in the countryside tread a tightrope: between access and conservation, involvement and interference, utilization and preservation. The NT and other organizations are dedicated to preserve our heritage, by ensuring access to certain areas while at the same time planning for the future. Walkers enjoy the highlights of the countryside at their leisure, but they owe it to themselves and others to conserve these pleasures for the generations to come. We have rights, but we also have responsibilities.

RIGHTS OF WAY AND ACCESS

Public footpaths, tracks and bridleways are 'public property' in the same sense as a road or car park. They are not owned by the public; however the landowner, while retaining rights of ownership, 'dedicates' a path or road to public use so that a right of way is established.

A right of way means the public is permitted to cross land by the designated route, without straying from it or causing undue damage. If you leave the path you may be trespassing; if you leave litter, or damage fences or crops, you lay yourself open to legal action. A right of way remains as such until it is revoked ('extinguished') in law, by the local authority. It is irrelevant how often the route is used, or whether it is overgrown, or blocked by a locked gate or a heap of manure. In some cases, however, rights of way may be diverted to permit buildings, roadworks or farming.

Footpaths and other public rights of way are indicated on the Ordnance Survey 1:50,000 (Landranger) series. In addition, public access is customary in common land since fencing it to keep people out is both legally complex and impractical.

Subject to the requirements of farming, forestry, private tenants and the protection of nature, the public is usually given free access to the NT's coast and

FOLLOW THE COUNTRY CODE

The Country Code helps you gain pleasure from the countryside while contributing to its care. Here are some of its main points:

1. Guard against all risk of fire.
2. Fasten all gates.
3. Keep dogs under close control.
4. Keep to public footpaths across farmland.
5. Use gates and stiles to cross fences, hedges and walls.
6. Leave livestock, crops and machinery alone.
7. Take litter home.
8. Help to keep all water clean.
9. Protect wildlife, plants and trees.
10. Take special care on country roads.
11. Make no unnecessary noise.

Above all:

12. Enjoy the countryside and respect its life and work.

country properties at all times. Of course the country code should be observed in these areas as well as elsewhere. Much of the NT's land is farmed, so take extra care to keep on paths in these areas. Details of NT-owned land are given in *Properties of the National Trust* and local publications.

BEWARE OF THE BULL
Complicated bye-laws cover release of bulls into fields crossed by a right of way. It is best to assume that any bull is potentially dangerous and to take a detour or avoid it if possible.

What to Wear

For all but the shortest routes the walker should be properly clothed. Purpose-designed boots and a waterproof top are not only sensible for comfort and safety, they also help you enjoy to the full your day out.

The first essential is some type of water- and windproof outer garment such as an anorak, cagoule or coat, preferably with a hood. Modern lightweight anoraks can be rolled and stowed away when not in use. For warmth the main requirement is several layers of insulating material such as woollen sweaters. These can be taken off as the weather improves, or added to if the wind strengthens. Wool 'breathes' to minimize sweating yet retains body heat effectively. A thick, warm shirt is also recommended.

Denim jeans are a bad choice for legwear. They are usually too restrictive and have poor insulating qualities. Walking trousers should be warm and comfortably loose to allow movement without chafing. On long walks carry waterproof overtrousers.

Feet are the walker's best friends, so care for them. Strong leather walking boots with studded or non-slip soles are the ideal choice. Good ankle support is a must in rocky and difficult terrain. For short walks on easy ground a pair of tough, comfortable shoes may be adequate. Wellingtons may be suited to very wet ground but quickly become uncomfortable and tend to rub up blisters. Whatever the footwear, thick woollen socks (two pairs, if possible) are the sensible choice beneath. Footwear *must be broken in* and fit comfortably before you take to the paths.

On longer walks it is wise to carry a few extras in your rucksack: a sweater, a spare pair of socks, a warm hat and a pair of woollen gloves.

▷ *The well-dressed walker pauses to consult the map. Many people new to rambling are surprised at how chilled they become after a couple of hours in the open air, away from warm rooms or the car heater. Even on sunny days the wind and a few hundred feet of altitude can make you feel uncomfortably cool. The moral: Be prepared!*

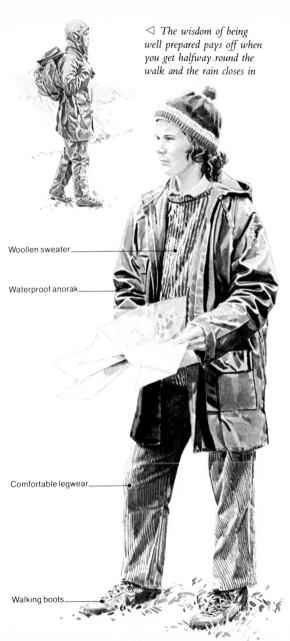

◁ The wisdom of being well prepared pays off when you get halfway round the walk and the rain closes in

Woollen sweater

Waterproof anorak

Comfortable legwear

Walking boots

What to Take

Certain items are basic to any respectable walk. A rucksack and good maps are vital. Other equipment depends on the nature of the walk and personal interests.

The rucksack or backpack has many advantages over a hand-carried bag. With a rucksack you can take more, carry it more comfortably, and leave your hands free (an important safety consideration in rough terrain). There is an enormous variety of rucksacks available. For a half-day or day walk choose a medium-sized model of about 20 litres capacity, made of nylon or similar, that fits you snugly without chafing.

A selection of maps should always be at hand. Do not rely solely on the sketch maps in this book. These sketch maps are intended for use with Ordnance Survey maps (1:50,000 *Landranger* series or, better, the *Outdoor Leisure Maps* and others at 1:25,000, about $2\frac{1}{2}$

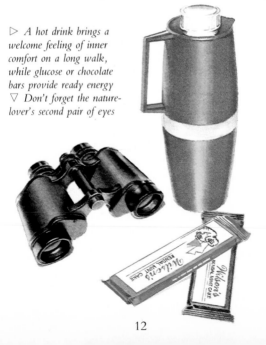

▷ *A hot drink brings a welcome feeling of inner comfort on a long walk, while glucose or chocolate bars provide ready energy*
▽ *Don't forget the nature-lover's second pair of eyes*

inches to the mile). A good map provides details of rights of way, viewpoints, parking, conveniences and telephones, and lets you identify distant features (see page 14). A compass is necessary for map-reading since paths are often indistinct or routes unmarked across open country. Local guidebooks and field guides point out items of interest as you go, rather than after you return.

On a long walk carry nourishment with you unless you are sure of a 'refuelling' stop. Concentrated high-energy food such as chocolate or mintcake revives flagging limbs and spirits, and a modern lightweight vacuum-flask provides a welcome hot beverage. A few sticking plasters, a penknife and a length of string may come in handy so keep them in a side pocket in your rucksack.

Walking is an excellent way of reaching an unusual viewpoint or approaching wary wildlife. A camera records the scene and 'collects' nature without damaging it, and binoculars permit close-ups of animals about their business. Walk with these items at the ready – you never know when they might be needed.

A compass is essential; a 35mm camera outfit is less so, though a pocket version may come in useful

Maps

A walker without a map is like a car without a steering wheel. It is essential to obtain good maps, learn how to read and interpret them, and check your route before you set off. Most experienced walkers use a combination of maps, as described below. The sketch maps in this book are not intended to be your sole guide: use them in combination with Ordnance Survey (OS) and other maps in guide books and local publications.

The OS maps come in two main scales. First is the *Landranger* 1:50,000 series (about $1\frac{1}{4}$ inches to the mile). These maps cover the entire country and show footpaths, bridleways, rights of way, farm buildings and other features. They are useful for general planning and for gaining an overall impression of the area.

The second main OS scale is 1:25,000 (roughly $2\frac{1}{2}$ inches to the mile). These maps are published as individual sheets of the *First* and *Second Series* covering the entire country, and as large fold-out *Outdoor Leisure Maps* for recreational areas, holiday regions and national parks. The 1:25,000 maps are often called the 'walker's maps' since they show features important to walkers and ramblers, such as field boundaries,

▽ *In the National Grid referencing system the first three numbers are the* Easting *(left to right), the second three numbers are the* Northing *(bottom to top), and the reference is accurate to within 100 metres (110 yards)*

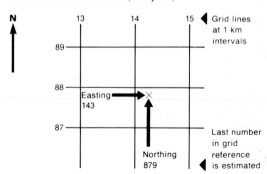

viewpoints, rescue posts and rights of way. Up-to-date 1:25,000 maps are recommended for use with the maps in this book. Further information is available from the Ordnance Survey (see address on page 127).

Another useful series is the *Footpath Maps* published by the Ramblers' Association (RA). These are at 1:25,000 scale and show many details such as footpaths, tracks, rides and bridleways, car parks and gates. For details of regions covered by these maps contact a local RA representative via a regional newspaper or community magazine, or enquire at the RA Head Office (for address see page 127).

Safety

Most of the routes described in this book can be completed safely by the average family, provided basic safety rules are observed. In more remote country, such as the Lake District, extra precautions are required.

1 Wear suitable clothing and footwear, as described in the previous pages.

2 Always assume the weather may suddenly turn nasty. Carry an extra sweater and an anorak, or cagoule, or even a small umbrella.

3 Obtain a good map and learn to read it. The maps in this book are intended for use in conjunction with detailed walkers' maps such as the Ordnance Survey 1:25,000 series.

4 On longer walks take some energy-giving food such as chocolate or glucose lozenges and a drink of some kind.

5 Allow plenty of time to complete your walk. A good average is two miles per hour, less if you enjoy views or watch nature at work.

6 If possible, have a first-aider in the group, and take change for emergency phone calls.

Lacock

A short sight-seeing walk, suitable for visitors to Lacock Abbey who wish to see some of the surrounding countryside. The route passes many old and beautiful cottages in Lacock village and also takes in the Fox Talbot Photographic Museum.

Visitors to the famous Lacock Abbey may wish to choose from two walks, either 2½m or an extended version of 4m, through the surrounding gentle countryside of the Avon Valley. The abbey, village, Manor Farm and Bewley Common are all NT-owned and there are endless attractions for those who appreciate historic rural architecture.

Leave the public car park at the back of the Red Lion, nearly opposite the entrance to Lacock Abbey, and turn left along High Street between attractive stone and half-timbered cottages of various centuries. Lacock Abbey is of course a 'must', to be visited now or at the end of the walk. The abbey was founded in the thirteenth century as an Augustinian nunnery and was subsequently converted into a Tudor dwelling house. It contains a copy of the 1225 Magna Carta (the original is in the British Museum) and there is also a very fine example of a sixteenth-century brewery in the grounds of the abbey.

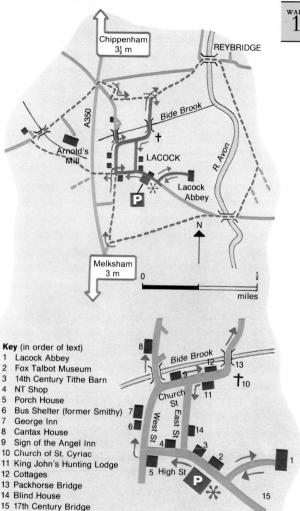

Chippenham
3½ m

REYBRIDGE

Bide Brook

A350

Arnold's Mill

LACOCK

Lacock Abbey

R. Avon

N

Melksham
3 m

0   ½
miles

Key (in order of text)
1   Lacock Abbey
2   Fox Talbot Museum
3   14th Century Tithe Barn
4   NT Shop
5   Porch House
6   Bus Shelter (former Smithy)
7   George Inn
8   Cantax House
9   Sign of the Angel Inn
10 Church of St. Cyriac
11 King John's Hunting Lodge
12 Cottages
13 Packhorse Bridge
14 Blind House
15 17th Century Bridge

Bide Brook

Church St

West St

East St

High St

Car park: Public parking by Lacock Abbey,
3m S of Chippenham and just E of A350.
Grid ref: ST 917 683.

◁ *The fourteenth-century tithe barn in Lacock village*

17

▷ ▷ *The approach to Lacock Abbey is bordered by some fine black walnut trees, whose fruit attracts squirrels and other nut-eaters; this species is a close relative of the common walnut*
▷ *The Sign of the Angel inn, in Lacock's Church Street. Lacock village and the abbey were donated to the NT in 1944 by Miss Matilda Talbot*

▽ *The George Inn, in Lacock's West Street*

Adjoining the abbey gates is a sixteenth-century barn, now the Fox Talbot Museum in honour of one of the inventors of photography and the former owner of the house (abbey). Next to this, on the corner of East Street, is the fourteenth-century Tithe Barn. Further down High Street is the NT shop, and at the bottom on the left is Porch House. Turn right past the war memorial into West Street and in 50y note the bus shelter on the left; it was formerly the village smithy.

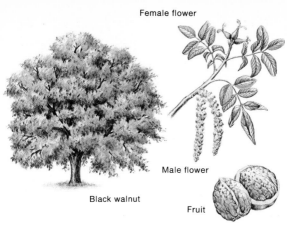

Female flower

Male flower

Black walnut

Fruit

Next door is the George Inn with a seventeenth-century spit that used to be turned by a dog.

Before turning right into Church Street, you might go forward a short distance over the eighteenth-century bridge spanning Bide Brook to see, a little farther along on the left, the beautifully-proportioned Cantax House (Georgian). Retrace your steps to Church Street and progress past the Sign of the Angel inn with its sixteenth-century doorway. Next is the square in front of the Church of St Cyriac where there is also King John's Hunting Lodge, a building believed to be even older than the abbey. One cottage in the row opposite has an unusual decoration of carved stone capitals under its eaves.

Turn left at the church, then in about 100y cross the ancient packhorse bridge. Keep along the path by the stream and up the hill to the end of the road. Here turn right on the tarmac path across a field to reach stone cottages at Reybridge. The path leads on to the road and on the left are thatched cottages with a Victorian (VR) pillar-box set in the wall by the road. Opposite is Rey Bridge spanning the Avon.

Pause as you cross the bridge to enjoy the fine views of the Avon flowing peacefully below. On the other side turn right immediately, over the stile, and strike diagonally left to the far corner where you rejoin the river and the swans sailing gracefully along. Climb over the wooden stile and keep to the riverbank for about 300y before negotiating another stile by the field gate. Cross the next field, following the telephone poles, and go through the next hedge by a stile about 20y to the right of the overhead lines. Continue straight on through the next stile, to the right of the farm gate, and now head almost due south towards the seventeenth-century road bridge over the Avon. As you cross this water meadow there are views of Lacock Abbey through the trees on the right.

Leave the peaceful water meadow through the field gate, turn right across the bridge and walk along the raised footpath. At the path's end turn quickly left, crossing the road to climb the stile into the field. Head to the right diagonally across the field, making for the end of the tall trees about two-thirds of the way along the hedge. As you pass through the gate to the next field keep along the hedgerow, past a line of mature oaks, in a general westerly direction. There is a caravan park before going over the wooden stile into the road.

The first section of the walk ends with 400y of road to the right, passing a garage and Lacock cricket ground to arrive at the west end of High Street. You may return along the High Street to the start, or if you are still game you can add an extension of about 1½m by walking a loop to the west.

Turn left through the stile by the signpost at the west end of the High Street, walk along the well-marked path through a field and through the gate to the busy

△ *Rey Bridge over the River Avon*
▷ *Lacock Abbey, its octagonal tower overlooking the calm River Avon*

Lacock bypass. Walk to the right for about 100y, cross the main road carefully and climb over the wooden stile. Now take a diagonal right direction to the corner of the field, over another stile and ahead to a third stile by a field gate. Cross the next field on the contour line, with the stream and Arnold's Mill beyond to the right. There is a stile again before you aim for the cottage on the other side of the next field, which you leave by the gate and turn right over the stone footbridge.

At the end of this causeway ignore the paths to left and right: instead continue ahead up a bank to a field stile. Follow the right fence north-east across the field, through a gate into a nursery (where the overgrown stile appears to be broken) and keep straight by the hedge until a stile leads into the road junction off the bypass to Lacock.

Cross over and walk along the road towards Lacock, in a short time reaching the village's name sign. Here turn left through a stile and then across the short field footpath, arriving at the hill end of the road above the packhorse bridge. Return to Lacock past the church and the left turn after King John's Hunting Lodge into East Street. Nearing the end of East Street and its junction with the High Street, on the left is the eighteenth-century lock-up. This is known as the 'Blind' house, since many of the overnight prisoners were drunks.

Selworthy

Selworthy and its hills, west of Minehead on the north Somerset coast, provide some of the most beautiful walking scenery in the country. This route is based on Selworthy village and includes an ascent to the beacon, rambles through the picturesque northern edge of Exmoor and views of the coastline and Porlock Marsh.

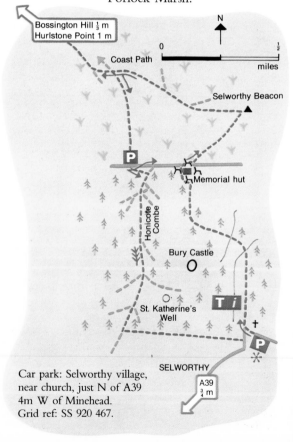

Bossington Hill ⅓ m
Hurlstone Point 1 m

Coast Path

N

0   ½
miles

Selworthy Beacon

P

Memorial hut

Honicote Combe

Bury Castle

St. Katherine's Well

T i

†

P

SELWORTHY

A39
¾ m

Car park: Selworthy village, near church, just N of A39 4m W of Minehead.
Grid ref: SS 920 467.

The whole of this walk is on NT land – the Holnicote Estate, donated to the NT in 1944 by Sir Richard Acland. Selworthy is one of the most picturesque and photographed villages in the country, and regularly appears on calendars. This 3m ramble (with a walk to Hurlstone Point that adds 1m) covers open heath and moor to the north of the village, with some woodland plus views on all sides from Selworthy Beacon (1,010f). The path is rough in places and stout footwear is essential.

The walk starts at the village car park, immediately below the church at the top of the village. The gleaming white church stands on high ground and can

△ △ *Looking back through the gate to Selworthy village green, at the start of the walk*
△ *The stony path at the beginning of the climb to the Beacon*

23

△ *The Memorial Hut provides shelter on the approach to Selworthy Beacon*
▷ *View from the Beacon. Selworthy is one of the main villages on the Holnicote Estate – over 12,000a of NT land taking in parts of north Exmoor, including Dunkery Beacon, and most of the land northwards to the coast. The moors around Dunkery, south of the A39 road, provide further excellent walking country*

be seen from a wide area. Largely sixteenth-century, with a fourteenth-century tower and superb windows, it is well worth a visit. So is the village, which has a fourteenth-century tithe barn in the rectory grounds. There are wonderful views from the church, south across Exmoor to Dunkery Beacon (the highest point on the moor).

West of the church, just off the road at the top of the village, is a gate. Go through this and in a few yards you reach the NT Information Centre and Shop, which should be visited for maps and booklets. Then walk up through the woods along the western end of the church. Go through a gate (NT sign) and take the right-hand, stony path, with a stream below on the left. Continue upwards to a sign *Selworthy Beacon* where you turn left, passing a 'bar'. The 'bars' are to prevent vehicles from wearing out the pathways.

After crossing two streams the going becomes softer, still winding up through the woods and eventually on to open moorland. The path now bears to the left, around and above the woods. Turn left at a signpost *Bury Castle* (an old iron-age hill fort which can be visited later in the walk, as an extra diversion). About 50y through the trees is the Memorial Hut,

erected in the late nineteenth century to the memory of
Sir Thomas Dyke-Acland (1787–1871). There are seats
on all four sides and it is possible to shelter here – from
the rain or sun!

One of the main points of the walk is Selworthy
Beacon and you can see this clearly from the hut,
northwards across the moor, with its trig-point
alongside it. Cross the narrow road and walk up a wide
track across the moor to the beacon. The summit is a
magnificent all-round viewpoint. On a clear day you
can see north-east across the Bristol Channel to the
Welsh coast; eastwards to North Hill, above
Minehead, and beyond to the Quantock Hills; south to
Dunkery Beacon and Exmoor; and west along the
coast to the Foreland and Countisbury Hill (above
Lynmouth).

After enjoying the view, take the path westwards
across the moor to a signpost *Coast Path*. Continue
straight on to enjoy another superb view across
Porlock Bay, Porlock village and the coastline beyond.
Buzzards and ravens sail overhead, and peregrines
sometimes nest on the cliffs. Down on Porlock Marsh
there are many waders, while skylarks, meadow pipits,
wheatears and curlews can be heard and seen. Heather,

*The curlew's plaintive
'meew' is a characteristic
sound of coast and open moor*

bracken and gorse cover the open parts of the moor, which turns royal purple in late summer.

Carry on westwards and shortly you meet a path which continues to Bossington Hill and Hurlstone Point. You have a choice here: a walk out to Hurlstone Point and back to this junction, which adds about 1m to the walk; or turn left now and return towards the Memorial Hut and Selworthy. On this path, fork right after a few yards on to the path back towards the trees. Along this section of the walk there are several rather odd-looking mounds. These were erected during the Second World War as ammunition bunkers and gun emplacements. American troops helped to build them, and also helped to build the road across the moor from North Hill, Minehead.

Arrive at the car park at the end of this road and the Memorial Hut is about 300y to the left, along the road; you can return via the hut and then down the path (up which you came) to Selworthy. The alternative is to walk eastwards along the path at the top of the wood for 200y then turn right along a track around a 'bar' and immediately fork right. (Bury Castle, ½m slightly leftwards, is another addition to this walk.) After forking right, cross an open space for 30y and turn left down a grassy path to the woods.

Continue straight ahead through a gate and down Holnicote Combe. The path is now quite steep and passes a *Selworthy Cross* sign on the right. Ignore this and a further 200y down there is another sign at a crossroads. Ignore this as well and continue straight ahead for 100y to a third signpost and take the left turn here, to *Selworthy* ½m along a path near the lower edge of the woods. In 300y, just by a small footpath on the left, is Katherine's Well – named after one of the Acland family. A spring has been enclosed to form the well, and just beyond is a post giving the well's name.

There is now a clear view to the right across Exmoor. In another 300y go straight across a wide track on to a narrow path through trees. Shortly the village and church appear close in front. Over a stile, turn right and you are on the village green; the NT Shop is there just below the church and the car park is nearby.

△ *Porlock Bay and towards Porlock village, from the moor*   ▽ *The charms of Selworthy beckon at the end of the walk*

Fontmell Down

The superb ridge downland between
Shaftesbury and Blandford Forum holds a
wealth of interest and beauty in its
wildflowers, grasses, butterflies and iron-age
cross-dykes. There are fine views over
Blackmoor Vale – Thomas Hardy's Dorset.

Fontmell Down, at the top of Spread Eagle Hill 3m
south of Shaftesbury, is part of the 280a of immaculate
chalk downland owned by the NT. On a sunny day in
early summer the scene is alive with the butterflies,
flowers and birds characteristic of chalk upland. Such
areas are now all too rare, so please take special care to
observe the country code and preserve these delights
for others on this 4m walk.

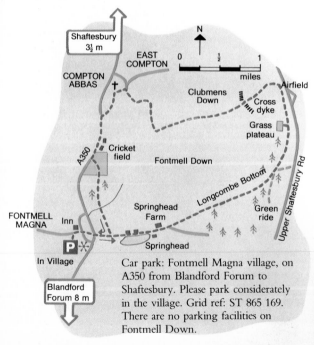

Car park: Fontmell Magna village, on
A350 from Blandford Forum to
Shaftesbury. Please park considerately
in the village. Grid ref: ST 865 169.
There are no parking facilities on
Fontmell Down.

Park with care in the village of Fontmell Magna. From the Crown Inn cross the A350 and take the lane, signposted *Ashmore*, leaving the Crown Garage on your right. Soon you pass a beautiful lake and a little farther on, at a sharp left-hand bend, a white thatched house on your right. This is Spring Head, once the home of the musician, writer and ecologist Rolf Gardiner; it is now a centre for the promotion of the arts and environmental study.

Just beyond the house is Springhead Farm on your left; a little farther on the road bends and on the left is a wide grass track. Turn off the lane on to this track and walk along it to a gate. Through the gate and straight across the next field, you come to a second gate with a stile beside it. Over the stile follow the track leading

△ *Spring Head, once home of writer Rolf Gardiner*
▽ *Looking north-east into Longcombe Bottom, a rounded valley*

uphill along the edge of a wood, with a wire fence on the right and the valley of Longcombe Bottom to the left. Ignore a tempting-looking stile in the fence on the right and keep steadily uphill until you emerge from the wood on to the open, sloping downland.

Half-right ahead is a faint grass track rising to a ridge of pine trees along the edge of a conifer wood. Follow this uphill until, in the angle of the fence facing you,

△ *Walking along the southern side of Longcombe Bottom, Fontmell Down rises across the valley to the north*
▽ *A wood 'hanger' on the skyline clings to Fontmell*

you see a gate with a stile. Enter the wood here and follow the narrow path through the undergrowth, still in the same north-easterly direction. The path turns very gradually to the right and eventually comes out on to a wide grass ride running left to right across you. Turn left on to the ride and continue along it to a gate at the end of the wood. The last part of this path is on a nature reserve owned by the Springhead Trust and leased to the Dorset Naturalists' Trust, so tread quietly.

Go through the gate and continue for a short distance along a grass track with the wood on your left until this comes to an end. Now you emerge out on to the downs. If you turn left to a little grass plateau where another path comes out from lower down, there is a superb view back down the valley of Longcombe Bottom. Leaving the plateau, continue round to your right along the top edge of a small bank, to the fence which runs away from you along the edge of the down. Keeping this fence on your right, follow it right round the top of the down, turning left along it at the far end, and go through the gate. The whole of this stretch is a permissive path granted by the NT in 1983, to avoid the walk along the Upper Shaftesbury road which is over to your right on the far side of the field.

Once through the gate you are on Fontmell Down proper. Turn half-right and climb up to the stile giving

The Blues Lycaenidae are the characteristic butterflies of chalk grassland. The upper wings have a bright blue surface, while the undersides are a dingy brown with blue streaks running to the wing roots

Small blue

Chalk-hill blue

Common blue

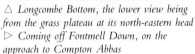

△ *Longcombe Bottom, the lower view being from the grass plateau at its north-eastern head*
▷ *Coming off Fontmell Down, on the approach to Compton Abbas*

entrance to the down from the road, by the NT plaque. Acquired in 1977 the 149a of unimproved downland is famous for butterflies, and contains iron-age cross-dykes. The public has access as far as the wood which crosses the tip.

Before moving on, pause and have a look round to your right. The swirl immediately to your right is Clubmens Down, and if you let your eye follow it round to the skyline, quarter-right you will be looking at Melbury Beacon. In 1804, when it was feared that Napoleon would invade England, Melbury Hill was the terminal post in a chain of signal beacons all along the Dorset coast. The ridge you are standing on is known as Fore Top. From behind you, and to your left, a long chalk ridge zig-zags its way south, down to the Stour valley at Child Okeford and then up again and along the eastern edge of Blackmoor Vale, along Bulbarrow and down to the River Piddle.

With the stile behind you, walk straight along the top of the ridge. Keep the wire fence on your right, until you come to a signpost at the end of the field,

pointing to Compton Abbas. Turn half-right and continue across the corner until you reach a fence where there is another NT plaque and a stile. Over the stile, turn left and walk along the right-hand side of the fence until you spot a descending grassy track down to your right. Leave the fence and follow a track down to a gate at the bottom of the hill.

Go through the gate and keep straight ahead with the trees on your left until a hedge and ditch cross at right-angles. Turn right along the hedge, keeping it on your left, until you come to a stile. Once over this you will be in a narrow lane running straight ahead. Follow it to the end and turn left into the road with the high wall of the Malt House on your left.

You are now in Compton Abbas, once the poor relation of East Compton which is about $\frac{1}{4}$m east. In days gone by East Compton had the church (its ruins are still there) and was the parish capital, and Compton Abbas was subtitled 'West Compton Up Fields'. The transfer of importance was undoubtedly due to the construction of the turnpike road (now the A350) in

1820. This ran through Compton Abbas north to south, whereas previously all major roads in the area had run east to west. Both Comptons were held by Shaftesbury Abbey at the time of the Domesday Book.

Follow the road through the village until you reach the main A350, turn left on to it and walk for about $\frac{1}{4}$m past Manor Farm and then two brick-and-flint cottages on the left. Just after the cottages is a signpost *Sutton Hill* and a stile on the left giving access to a cricket field. Cross the stile and keep left round the end of the field until you come to a small copse on your left. Turn into this and continue straight through to another stile. Over this, turn right along the hedge and walk almost to the end of the field. Then leave the hedge, go through a gate on the right, straight ahead and through a second gate, then over a brook and into the next field.

You are now nearly back at the start. Make for the high black barn and farm buildings on the right; negotiate two stiles and a ditch, cross the field diagonally left to a stile; over this and turn right into the lane. At the end of the lane is the Crown Inn.

Fontmell Magna itself repays a leisurely visit. It is a very picturesque village, enlivened by the Fontmell Brook wriggling through it and with one of the finest

churches in the county. Two of the six bells in the church are pre-Reformation and it has a sixteenth-century linenfold screen and a fifteenth-century tower with a nineteenth-century topknot.

The village is mentioned – as 'Funtamel' – in the oldest West Saxon charter of which a good text survives. Until 1978 Fontmell boasted a 'Gossip Tree' – a massive elm with seats round it, believed to have been 250 years old when it became diseased and had to be felled.

△ Brick-and-flint construction, with the flintstones sandwiched between layers of redbrick. The carefully-tended brookside garden is typical of many in the area

◁ Grassy track along the downland ridge towards the end of the route, with fine views over photogenic Dorset

Lambert's Hill Forts

A three-part walk taking in three NT historic sites north of Lyme Regis, Dorset. Lambert's Castle Hill, Coney's Castle and Pilsdon Pen all bear iron-age forts in varying degrees of preservation and from Pilsdon, highest point in Dorset, the views are breathtaking. There are short drives between each site.

This triple walk consists of three NT properties, each offering delightful short rambles of a mile or two. All three sites can be walked quite easily in one day, or even during a long afternoon. A short car drive is necessary between each of the properties; the order in which you visit them is immaterial.

Lambert's Castle Hill and Coney's Castle are almost adjacent, about 3–4m north-west of Lyme Regis, Dorset; Pilsdon Pen is a further 3m east towards Broadwinsor. Choose a clear day for the outing and you will be rewarded with some of the finest views on the south coast.

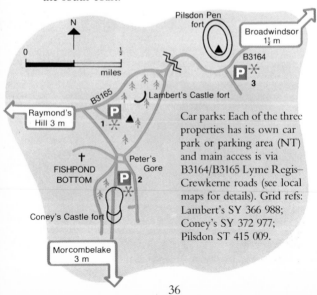

Car parks: Each of the three properties has its own car park or parking area (NT) and main access is via B3164/B3165 Lyme Regis–Crewkerne roads (see local maps for details). Grid refs: Lambert's SY 366 988; Coney's SY 372 977; Pilsdon ST 415 009.

Lambert's Castle Hill property covers 167a so there is scope for a ramble of 1m or so. This could be across the flat grass-covered centre, and provided one does not go downhill off the summit (842f) then the car park is never more than $\frac{1}{2}$m away. Down to the east is Chesil Bank, while Dartmoor looms in the far west.

A right turn at the end of the central track from the car park leads along a little path through gorse and bracken. This becomes a wider path with Marshwood Vale to the left. Continue, ignoring a track going downhill, and for a return to the car park bear right towards the centre and as you come to the main track make for the gate and car park. Not much is left of the round barrow or iron-age hill fort and the line of the ramparts is a little obscure.

Coney's Castle is also an ancient hill fort and is just south of Lambert's Castle Hill. On the drive from Lambert's to Coney's there is a little white church of St John the Baptist, without tower or steeple, to be seen at Fishpond.

The site of Coney's Castle, only 86a, is a gem. Nature has been left undisturbed, apart from a maintained grassy path across the centre. Here and there are patches of Himalayan balsam, blooming in July; although not indigenous this plant has been here

△ *The flat, grassy summit of Lambert's Castle Hill*

37

long enough to be included in our wildflower books. In high summer butterflies seem everywhere and one of our less common species, the small copper, may well be seen.

The hill fort was built about 500 BC in frontier country between the Dumnonii tribe, who gave their name to Devon, and the Durotriges tribe living in what we now call Wessex. Earth banks still remain. This may have been Egbert's fort when he fought the Danes in AD 833.

The walk around the fort is under 1m. From the car park follow the arrows to the road and go over a stile. Take the path across the grassy centre and, on coming to the end, double back round to the left. This leads along the ditch outside the rampart, which in spring is carpeted with bluebells. Beeches line the perimeter and the gaps between them give wide views east over Marshwood Vale. The path leads back to the car park.

From Lambert's or Coney's the drive to Pilsdon Pen is about 4m, east towards Broadwindsor. A stile and a gate are across the B3164 road from the car park. Go straight ahead, uphill, with a fence on left and follow the path to the 905f summit of the Pen. The climb is not as severe as it looks.

From the trig-point the scene is breathtaking – so is the wind at times. Due south across Marshwood Vale is Golden Cap (NT) with the sea both east and west. If conditions are right, local folk say that the glint of sun on water in the far north-west enables one to see the Bristol Channel. About 2m east is Lewesdon Hill,

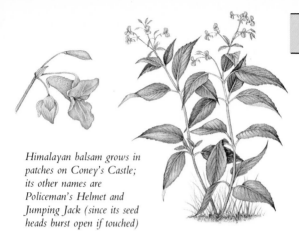

Himalayan balsam grows in patches on Coney's Castle; its other names are Policeman's Helmet and Jumping Jack (since its seed heads burst open if touched)

another NT property. Years ago as sailors drew into Lyme Bay, they dubbed the two hills of Pilsdon and Lewesdon 'The Cow and The Calf'. To the east is Chesil Beach and the Devon coast fades westwards.

The wide central area of the Pen stretches northwards from the trig-point, and you keep straight ahead towards the ramparts. The hill fort is 'multi-vallate', that is, it has more than one ditch and rampart. On the farthest of these there is a path round the fortifications and back to the summit, a distance of less than 1m.

◁ *The sleeping fields of Dorset, from Coney's Castle hilltop*
▽ *The view from Pilson Pen, Dorset's highest hill*

Cerne Giant

The highlight of this moderate ramble is the NT's archaeological property, the Cerne Abbas Giant cut in chalk downland in central Dorset. Besides this historical curiosity the walk includes beautiful views over the valley from the hill rising above the little River Cerne.

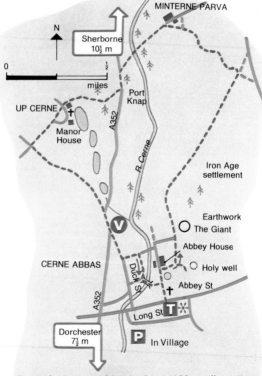

Car park: Street parking in Cerne Abbas village, 7m N of Dorchester just off A352 (to Sherborne). Take care parking in street. Grid ref: ST 666 011.

The ancient Cerne Giant is a hill-figure of a 'vigorous' man cut deep into the chalk downland, and like similar figures is best viewed from afar or on postcards. For a long time the Giant has been regarded as Romano-British, probably Hercules, but recent research suggests that he is much earlier and might well be an iron-age deity. The walk is about $4\frac{1}{2}$m long.

The start of the walk is Cerne Abbas – once a busy market town, but now a charming village. Long Street (the main street) or Duck Street are probably the best parking places. Be careful not to obstruct any entrance. For those who only wish to see the Giant, the suggested

▷ *A timbered house in Abbey Street, Cerne Abbas. Timber-framed buildings are unusual in the county; the marble and stone quarries, particularly around Portland, yielded high quality material that has become world famous*
▽ *Abbey House, its name recalling the now-ruined but still impressive Benedictine abbey to the north of the village. The abbey has gone, but the pagan giant still looks down on its remains*

route is along Duck Street to the Giant Viewpoint, on the A352. The return can be as in the $4\frac{1}{2}$m ramble, described below.

Start by walking north from Long Street along Abbey Street, where there are some fine houses. Note especially the timbered building, which is unusual for Dorset. The tower of St Mary's Church is a dominant feature and if you are interested in old churches a visit might prove worthwhile. Ahead is the lovely Abbey House and for a small sum you can visit the gateway of this one-time important Benedictine Abbey, founded in AD 987 and remaining until the Dissolution.

Just beyond the duckpond go through an iron gate on the right into the churchyard. Before continuing the route, which is along the left-hand path, take the right track by the side of a tile-roofed wall and walk down a little slope to view St Augustine's Holy Well, once part of the abbey.

Return and continue to a fork where the left-hand path crosses the churchyard and leads to another iron gate beneath an arch. Pass through the arch into a meadow. Make for the left end of trees until you meet a track. Bear left along this track for only a short distance to the wooden fences on each side, with large blue gates at each end of the fences. Pass through the first gate and then through a kissing gate at the end of the right-hand fence. From here the path goes slightly uphill to a stile; over this, climb uphill and round to the left until you reach the NT sign *Cerne Abbas Giant*.

△ *Walking out of Cerne Abbas, up towards the Giant's hill*
◁ *Cerne Abbas churchyard and the tower of St Mary's*

The Giant is inside a wire fence enclosure – not that he is likely to escape – and of course you cannot get a clear view of him from this side of the valley. Take one of the grassy paths parallel to the protective fence above and the hedge below; keep to this along the side of the hill. There are several such paths and it does not really matter which one you take, so long as you are heading north. Gradually you climb the side of the hill, and as higher ground is gained so the path bears a little right and then steeply up to scrub – mostly hawthorn and bramble – that signals the approaching summit. The humps and bumps of this scrub are in fact remains of early earthworks and doubtless have some connection with the folk who carved out the Giant.

There should be a fence and stile ahead. On the stile and looking at right-angles from the fence into the still-rising field, the top of a barn can just be seen half-left, peeping above the brow. Descend from the stile and walk the right of way across the field to the barn, but if there is a standing crop it is possible to follow the hedge round the field to the barn. Whichever line you take, pass through a gate on to a track so that trees are to the left and barn on the right. Pass through a Hampshire gate, which is simply poles and wire with the free end tied or looped to a standing post. After $\frac{1}{4}$ m turn left on to a path through a gap in the hedge. Take a course slightly right of centre over a field, downhill, to a large blue iron gate and through on to open chalk hillside.

Chalk supports a distinctive selection of plants and animals, particularly the beautiful small flowers. In midsummer, yellow hawksbeard covers the downland and close to the earth there is wild thyme and bedstraw. Here and there on a July day the rare bee and pyramid orchids may be found – definitely not to be picked, of course. Butterflies abound including tortoiseshells, browns, heaths and the beautiful blues characteristic of chalk grassland, while day-flying burnet and cinnabar moths – not easily recognised as such – take their share of the blossoms.

After the blue iron gate a winding track leads ahead downhill, through another blue gate, and makes for a solitary tree ahead. After the tree the footpath becomes a cart track which merges with a better-defined stony road. Go through a gate where there is a house ahead and turn right. Follow this farm road round to the left and down to the little hamlet of Minterne Parva. Note a very old circular farm building and the stump and plinth, probably from a village cross.

The way is now a surfaced road, dropping downhill through wooded banks where hart's-tongue ferns and ramsons (wild garlic) grow in profusion in their seasons. You may just catch the sound of tumbling water from a tiny stream before rising to meet the

tarmac and traffic of the main A352 road.

Turn left along the road for only a few hundred yards and on coming to a signpost – *Pot Knap* – take a right for Up Cerne. Although this is a metalled road there should be little traffic, which allows you to admire the magnificent beeches on both sides. Up Cerne is real, not a dream: there are a few cottages, a church, a manor house, and the little River Cerne with its crystal-clear water flowing southwards towards Frome.

Just beyond the cottages go straight ahead, passing the church on the left. As you climb the hill, pause to look back at the beautiful manor house. Follow the road until it turns left and then continue back to the A352. It is only a short distance right (south) along the main road to the Giant Viewpoint, from where the Giant stands erect across the valley. The grim and forbidding building on the right is the workhouse of Victorian Cerne Abbas.

Bear left away from the A352 along the road to the village. (Walkers on the short route join at this point.) Take the first left and, on coming to the River Cerne, turn right along a footpath beside the stream. This leads back to Cerne Abbas, with a footbridge to Abbey Street or the other way to Mill Lane and Duck Street.

△ *Male fern and a frond alongside the hart's tongue fern*
◁ *The impressive Giant carved into the hillside chalk*

45

Stiles

'Jog on, jog on, the footpath way,
And merrily hent the stile – a.'

That quotation from the song by Autolycus in Shakespeare's *The Winter's Tale* indicates that stiles have been in existence since the early seventeenth century, and probably for much longer. Things have progressed, however, to the point where there is now a British Standards Institution specification for stiles!

A stile (derived from the old English *stingel* – to climb) is a term that covers any man-made means of enabling people – but not animals – to get through or over a fence, hedge or wall other than by using a gate. For most of us the word immediately brings to mind the standard design of the *bar-and-step stile* (or *three-barred step stile*) – three horizontal wooden rails fixed to two uprights, about four feet high and the same distance apart, with a step under the middle rail protruding on both sides. Although this is by far the commonest type of stile, there are many interesting and unusual variations that make 'stile-spotting' an

▽ *The common bar-and-step stile*
▷ *Ladder stiles are fine for humans but defeat most dogs*

absorbing adjunct to country rambles.

In areas where fields are divided by stone walls you may come across a wooden trestle or ladder, perhaps with a vertical pole at the top as a hand-grip. This *ladder stile* enables you to climb over the wall without damaging either the wall or yourself. Another variation in stone-wall country consists of pieces of stone jutting out at intervals from the wall, forming steps up (or down) both sides of the wall. This *step stile* is practical but you have to be careful not to graze your legs if wearing shorts or a skirt.

Another type of stile is the *V stile*. This consists of pieces of timber or stone either set at, or making, an angle with just enough room near the ground for the lower parts of the average human body to pass through – but not animals. An example of this type of stile can be seen on the pathway up the NT-owned Glastonbury Tor in Somerset.

Finally (but by no means comprehensively) there is the turnstile. For most people this is possibly associated more with sports grounds and supermarkets but it is still to be found in the countryside. Depending on its design, this sort of stile usually acts as a barrier but only to larger animals. The NT provides a good example, alongside the main gateway to Stourhead House.

▷ *The V stile or step stile allows two-legged creatures, such as ourselves, to pass but bars the four-legged ones*
▽ *The turnstile is now a rare sight in the countryside Step stile built in a stone wall* ▽

Ringmoor & Turnworth

Ringmoor is the site of a remarkably
preserved Romano–British settlement
surrounded by deciduous woodland in central
Dorset, west of Blandford Forum. There are
fine views from Turnworth Down of the
surrounding chalk uplands and scenery.

The fine downlands and farm country west of
Blandford Forum provide the setting for this 5m walk.
The NT's Ringmoor site, on Turnworth Down,
contains well-preserved remains of settlements dating
from the centuries on either side of the Roman
conquest.

Leave the car park by the stile in the corner farthest
from the road and turn right on to a stony lane running
uphill. After about 100y there is a large barn on the
right and just beyond it is the Okeford Picnic Site off to
the right. This is indicated by a large arrow and reached
by climbing the stile and crossing a field. From it, and
from the lane itself, there is a superb view right across

△ *About ½m out from the start, a grassy cart
track curls round hedgerow trees and shrubs with
Ringmoor settlement, which contains interesting
and well preserved remains, to the left*
▷ *Looking across the agricultural land of
Ibberton Long Down, on the south-easterly
section of the route*

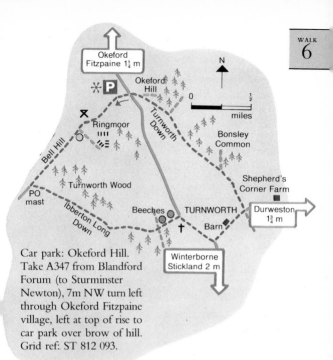

Okeford
Fitzpaine 1¼ m

Okeford
Hill

N

0   ½
miles

Turnworth
Down

Bonsley
Common

Ringmoor

Bell Hill

Shepherd's
Corner Farm

Turnworth Wood

PO
mast

Durweston
1¾ m

Ibberton Long
Down

Beeches

TURNWORTH

Barn

Winterborne
Stickland 2 m

Car park: Okeford Hill.
Take A347 from Blandford
Forum (to Sturminster
Newton), 7m NW turn left
through Okeford Fitzpaine
village, left at top of rise to
car park over brow of hill.
Grid ref: ST 812 093.

Blackmoor Vale and, over on the right, to Duncliffe Hill, Shaftesbury, Melbury Beacon and Fontmell Down.

For a short section the lane becomes a grassy cart-track, with thickish scrub on the left, and a large dewpond. This is the entrance to Ringmoor, acquired by the NT in 1978. Here the outlines of a Romano-British settlement and its fields can be traced on the ground. The small circular banks are probably the site of the farmers' settlement, with radiating tracks leading out to a network of small fields round about.

Shortly after the entrance to Ringmoor the track becomes stony again, and the view begins to open out. Straight ahead you can see the ends of the three ridges which run along either side of the Piddle and Cerne

◁ The tower of St Mary's, Turnworth, marks the walk's halfway point
▽ Holly trees were often planted to indicate parish boundaries. The trees are either male or female, as evidenced by their flowers; a tree that never bears berries is either male, or a female too far from her male neighbours to be pollinated
▷ Holly and bramble on the approach track to Bonsley Common

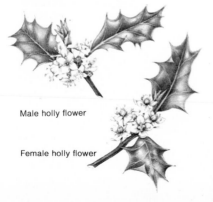

Male holly flower

Female holly flower

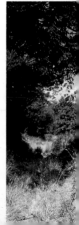

valleys. The track you have been walking along since the car park is a section of what is believed to be a branch of the Great Ridgeway, one of the oldest roads in Britain, dating back to the stone age and thought to have run from East Anglia to Devon.

When the lane emerges from the scrub into the open, on your left is a small hut with a Post Office mast. Turn left, leaving the hut on your right, and walk along the flint and grass track with a hedge on the left and a post-and-wire fence on the right. After a few minutes you pass another little hut on your right and soon the track becomes entirely grass and begins to go gradually downhill. Then the fence on your right finishes and you are walking along the top edges of two fields which slope down to the right. All the way along this section of the walk the views ahead of you are widening and on a clear day you should be able to see across to the Purbeck Hills on the coast. To the right is a fascinating series of rolling downs and 'bottoms', as these roadless, rounded valleys are called.

The track ends when the hedge on your left turns right to cross it, and there is a small bridle gate ahead. Go through this and walk out on to the field. Turn half-left, walk straight across the field to the opposite corner and go through the gate on the right (ignoring a tempting stile in the hedge on your left). You are looking into a large cultivated field, which drops away with a belt of trees at the far end. In the foreground are two solitary trees and a telephone line. Take a bearing from where you stand to a point halfway between the trees and the telephone post and walk straight along

this bearing to the far end of the field. Here you will find either a gap in the fence or a gate, with a stile beside it. Walk through, cross a grass track running from left to right and pass a field entrance on your right. Continue straight ahead down a narrow grass path with a hedge on the right and three splendid beech trees on the left. Follow this path down to the Okeford–Turnworth road.

Turn right and walk along the road through Turnworth village, passing St Mary's Church (restored under the architectural supervision of Thomas Hardy) on your right. At the far end of the village the road bears gently to the right and, just as it is about to enter a flattened S-bend, you see a wooden bridleway signpost to Durweston on your left. Follow its direction up the stony lane, passing a large barn on the left, and take the right fork to follow the telephone line. At the top of the hill a grassy lane, with a wood at the end of it, comes in from the left. Turn along this and you are walking along the parish boundary, as evidenced by the half-dozen or so old holly trees

surviving in the hedge on your left. If you stop half-way along the hedge and then turn round and look half-right ahead, you will see Shepherds Corner in the dip. This was once a great junction of many ancient roads and trackways. On the right are the mixed woodlands of Bonsley Common.

The track continues into the wood, in the same north-westerly direction, so keep straight ahead as you enter and follow the track through to the far end. Go through the gate and you emerge on to an open down, dropping steeply downhill on the left and with a thick gorse hedge on the right. Continue straight ahead, keeping the gorse on your right, through a gate at the far end and carry on in the same direction to a second gate which gives access to a stony lane. Above, to the north, is Okeford Hill. Turn left here and walk down-hill along the lane to the road and, half-right ahead on the other side, the car park.

◁ *Thorns old and new: holly and barbed wire*
▽ *Entering the woodland of Bonsley Common, on the home leg*

Gasper Mill

A varied walk based on the NT's Stourhead Estate, Wiltshire, in truly rural scenery with woods, open farmland and fine views. The route provides an opportunity to see some of the lesser-known features of the area such as Bonham, Pen Pits, Gasper Mill and New Lake.

The NT's Stourhead property covers 2,645a and includes landscaped pleasure gardens and lakes, Stourhead House containing fine collections of furniture and art, and the village of Stourton; plus woodland, neolithic barrows, an iron-age hill fort and unspoilt downland. This 5m walk takes you into some less-frequented parts of the estate and is generally easy going apart from one steep and usually muddy ascent. (Walks 9 and 12 are also based at Stourhead.)

Leave the main Stourhead car park by the exit to the house and gardens. Go down the slope and, at the point where the fence ends on the left, turn left by a rustic seat on to an unmade path with a barbed-wire fence on your right. (Do not go through the gate on your right.) From this unmade path there are views over the

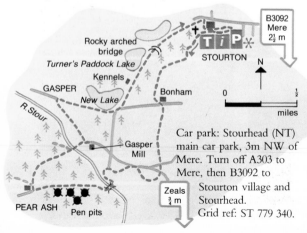

Car park: Stourhead (NT) main car park, 3m NW of Mere. Turn off A303 to Mere, then B3092 to Stourton village and Stourhead.
Grid ref: ST 779 340.

NT Offices at Stourton village, Stourton Church and Stourhead Gardens. When you are almost at the eastern end of the church, look out for a short length of track on the left leading to a gate. Take this track, go through the gate, turn right and follow the side of the wood to the corner of the field. Turn left at this point, and make for a double stile ahead. Over the stiles, turn right and again following the side of the wood make for a small gate that gives access to an open field. From this field you should have distant views of Bulbarrow Hill, Duncliffe Hill, Melbury Beacon and the town of Shaftesbury.

Head for some farm buildings on the other side of the field. Soon you see a fence running down to the right from the farm buildings. Go through a gate a short distance down this fence and, turning very slightly left, make for and go through another gate in the fence on your left, at the point where a thick hedge starts. Turn right into the farm road which leads to a minor metalled road, where a left turn brings you alongside Bonham House.

Part of this house was the former Roman Catholic chapel of St Benedict, which was deconsecrated some years ago. After the Reformation this chapel became a small stronghold of Roman Catholicism and the Catholics in the area used to come here to worship. A bell lantern on the roof bears witness to its former use.

Almost immediately opposite the gate to Bonham

△ Stourton Church, with the gardens of Stourhead behind

△ *Wildflowers jostle in the two hedges flanking the lane running south from Bonham House. The views on this section gradually widen to include Duncliffe Hill and White Sheet Hill and the village of Shaftesbury*

▽ *The wooden bridge spanning the River Stour, dammed by Henry Hoare II* ▷▽ *Beware summer foliage and blooms obscuring route markers, as with the white gate just after crossing the Stour*

House, take the green lane hedged on both sides. Through gaps in the left-hand hedge there are pleasant views and, from the point where the hedge on the left ends, there are even more impressive views of Duncliffe Hill, Shaftesbury and White Sheet Hill.

Follow the hedge on the right to a gate which leads to a short length of unmade road. At this point turn right and, crossing the road running from left to right, take the narrow metalled road in front which leads down through the hamlet of White Cross. Keep going to the left and ignore all roads to the right. The road descends fairly steeply, bears round to the left and eventually leads down the valley to where the infant River Stour runs cool between shady banks.

Follow the river for a short distance, cross south over the wooden bridge and then, just before a white gate, turn right up a track. This is the steepest and almost certainly the muddiest part of the walk, and those who ignored advice about stout footwear will find themselves ankle-deep in trouble. Do not be tempted off this track by one which leads to the right. As you climb through the wood, on either side are the sites of some of the thousands of Pen Pits found in the

area. These were originally thought to be the remains of a large settlement, but in 1883 the archaeologist General Pitt-Rivers carried out excavations and established that they were in fact small quarries, dating from 1800 BC, from which lumps of greensand were excavated and made into grindstones and whetstones.

As the path levels off it begins to leave the wood until you eventually emerge on to a metalled road at Pear Ash. Turn almost immediately right, past an attractive cottage on the left, and follow a track leading back into woodland around a single horizontal pole barrier (ignore the track going left just after the barrier). As you go straight ahead the track descends fairly steeply, and about halfway down the slope cross over another track that comes in sharply from the left and goes to the right. As you emerge from the wood the track converges with another coming in from the left; turn right and walk on to Gasper Mill, which has been converted into a private house.

Just before the outbuildings of the mill there is a gate on the left. Go through it and follow the right-hand hedge along the old county road (now a grass path)

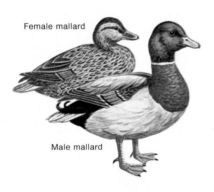

Female mallard

Male mallard

△ *Mallard abound on the lakes at Stourhead. The seductively-coloured male stands in front of a drab-brown female*
▷ *Walking downhill from Gasper, New Lake is on the left. The lakes of Stourhead were produced artificially in a shallow, fertile valley known as Six Wells Bottom, watershed of three rivers — one being the Dorset Stour*

appropriately known as Mill Lane. Shortly you go through a second gate into another stretch of green lane with hedges on both sides. This lane leads to a metalled road where there are a few houses and cottages – the hamlet of Gasper.

Turn right on to the road and head down the hill. At the bottom is New Lake on your left – a favourite spot with anglers and ducks (mainly mallard). Follow the road to a junction and bear left (signed *Stourton*). You soon see on your left two small lakes with an unusually-shaped building between them. The building, with compounds on either side, was the Kennels for the packs of hounds kept by former owners of Stourhead House, and is still known by that name. Following The Kennels is a rocky, arched bridge, Turner's Paddock Lake (on the left) and shortly afterwards the village of Stourton and its church are back in view. Pause here to enjoy the Spread Eagle pub or seasonal refreshments in the village hall, and the NT Shop in the pub courtyard. Finally make your way through the pub car park back up the hill to the main car park and the start.

Studland

A coastal and chalk hill walk around Studland
Bay and Peninsula south-west of
Bournemouth. The route passes through
several NT sites in an area of outstanding
natural beauty famous for its downs and sandy
heaths, one of which – Godlingston Heath – is
a national nature reserve.

This moderate 6m ramble is over well-defined paths
across large tracts of NT land. The route includes
Studland village and the bay itself, Old Harry Rocks,
Ballard Down and Godlingston Heath (now a national
nature reserve). There are no refreshments obtainable
en route other than the pub at the start, so you would
be wise to carry a packed lunch. The walk can be
reduced to 3½m by the short-cut from Ballard Down
back to Studland.

Studland village is worth exploring, either before or
after the walk. Its church is one of the oldest in Dorset
with much early Norman work. The first Christian

△ *The easily-eroded sandy paths on Godlingston Heath*

Little Sea

Toll road to ferry

Godlingston
Heath

Agglestone

Golf course

B3351

Corfe
astle 4 m

Dean Hill

Obelisk

Swanage
1¾ m

STUDLAND

Studland Bay

Handfast Pt

Old Harr
Rocks

Old Nick's
Ground

The Pinnacle

Ballard Down

Ballard Pt

N

0   ½   1
miles

Swanage Bay

Car park: NT parking
adjacent to Bankes Arms,
Studland, via either
Sandbanks Ferry or
A351/B3351 from Wareham.
Grid ref: SZ 037 825.

shrine here was built by St Aldhelm, probably in the
seventh century, and there are still traces of his Saxon
walls. The village cross, not far from the church, has a
stone base possibly as old. Since 1976 there has been a
modern cross on the base. The new cross's east side
shows Christ surmounting a miscellany of objects
including a violin, a bomb, a butterfly, and Concorde;
the west side depicts Man as a hunter, with a vine and
birds; and the other sides are equally fascinating if
somewhat enigmatic.

From the car park at Studland turn right to pass the
Bankes Arms. At the bottom of the hill, where the
road bears right, turn left on to a bridleway signposted
Swanage via Old Harry. This track leads eastwards to
Old Harry Rocks. On the way there are fine views of
Studland Bay to the left, and across the bay are the high
buildings of Bournemouth. In midsummer corn
marigolds shine bright in the growing corn and the air
is alive with swooping and diving sand martins.

△ *Old Harry, the Devil himself, watches over Studland Bay and Poole Harbour*

Suddenly you emerge from a wood on to the headland, Handfast Point, to be confronted by the sea. You are at the end of the east-west chalk ridge that forms the Purbeck Hills. Below are great stacks of chalk cut by sea erosion. One stack is Old Harry, who is of course the Devil himself. Another stack – once known as Old Harry's Wife – collapsed many years ago. Straight ahead across the sea you may see, if visibility allows, another great white chalk promontory which rises above the Needles on the Isle of Wight. In prehistoric times there was no sea and the line of chalk was continuous.

The path follows the coastline round the right, that part nearest to Old Harry being known as Old Nick's Ground. There follows a gradual climb south-west to Ballard Point. *It is very dangerous* to go near the cliff edge, especially on windy days, and young children should be kept on the path. As you gradually walk upwards take a backward look to see the chalk cliffs and the Pinnacle rocks below.

At Ballard Point leave the coast's edge and take the path round to the right alongside a wire fence, keeping along the ridge to pass a trig-point. Farther on a gate leads to the NT property of Ballard Down and beyond this, at another gate, there is also a gate into a field on the right. Here you can rest on a large stone seat, inscribed *Rest and Be Thankful*. The view is truly

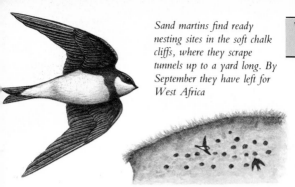

Sand martins find ready nesting sites in the soft chalk cliffs, where they scrape tunnels up to a yard long. By September they have left for West Africa

magnificent. To the south is the sweep of Swanage Bay, with Durlston Head jutting out into the sea; northwards is Poole Harbour and its islands; Poole Bay stretches for miles until it fades away along the Hampshire coastline. The large wooded island in the harbour is Brownsea (NT-owned). Westwards lie the Purbeck Hills with Nine Barrow Down just visible beyond Ballard. Whitecliff, which is signposted, is another NT property adjacent to Ballard Down.

(The walk may be shortened at this point by passing the stone seat and taking the diagonal track across the field, downhill to Studland Cross, where you turn right for the car park at the start.)

The route continues westwards along the hills and after ¾m there is an obelisk to commemorate the first water supply to Swanage. Beyond this obelisk the track bears right and then downhill to a road, where you turn left. Continue along the road to a stile on the right. Cross over and make for another stile which can be seen in a fence half-right up the hill, Dean Hill. Should foliage make it difficult to spot this stile, take a half-right direction until the stile can be seen. Cross this next stile and continue up Dean Hill along a narrow path winding through a little wood. At the top there is an old, disused building on the right and a golf course ahead. The right of way crosses the course, but watch for players and keep your ears open for shouts of 'Fore!'. Stay near the left hedge, but as higher ground is reached the hedge ends and you should follow a narrow gully to a large bar-type gate. This leads on to the Studland-Corfe Castle road. Turn right and (as usual) walk in single file because of traffic.

After only 200y of road watch out for a wooden signpost on the right, pointing north across the road to the Agglestone. This sign may be hidden by trees, but on the north side of the road there is also a stone indicator to the Agglestone. Follow the bridleway signs indicating the right of way, which is in the same general direction as the signs except for twists and turns of the track. You are on Godlingston Heath, and the deep sandy paths are subject to constant weathering by wind and rain. At a wider crossing track, turn left and make for the Nature Conservancy notice board on higher ground to the left. Follow this path to the Agglestone.

The massive Agglestone rock is ferruginous (iron-containing) sandstone and is said to weigh over 400 tons. It stands on a barrow and its name probably comes from 'hag', Anglo-Saxon for a witch or fiend, and 'stan' meaning stone; another possibility is 'Eggelstan', meaning a sharp or sticking-up stone. It was possibly a rock–deity in prehistoric times. There is an old legend that the Devil threw the stone from the Isle of Wight in order to demolish Corfe Castle, but obviously he did not throw it far enough.

On the other side of the stone go downhill along a very sandy path, over a causeway across several

streams. These feed Little Sea (glimpses of which are to the east), a large area of fresh water on Studland Heath between the ferry road and the sea. The lake is a haven for numerous birds.

If you are on the heath in summer look out for the beautiful blue heath milkwort, and by the little causeway bridge over the stream it is not difficult to find the common sundew, which traps and digests tiny insects. White cottongrass in the bogs blows with the wind and also in midsummer there is the yellow star-like bog asphodel.

There are a number of paths on the heath, but you bear to the right with a hillock on the left. Soon after passing the hillock the track merges with another; bear right with this, and it soon becomes a clear wide path. The direction is now south-east for the return to Studland. Pass through woodland to a little stream, which can be crossed on the stones, and then go right and slightly uphill, still in the wood. This path soon becomes a wide gravel road with a few houses, and it leads directly to the ferry road at Studland. As you approach the village turn right, and take the first left then immediately first right for the Bankes Arms and (if your timing is right) a thirst-quenching end to this invigorating and charming walk.

◁ *Handfast Point, at the eastern end of the Purbecks*
▽ *The Agglestone stands on an ancient barrow on Godlingston Heath. Note the deep-cut paths through the heather, exposing the sandy subsoil beneath. Heathland is particularly susceptible to damage by carelessly-placed boots, so please keep to the tracks here*

Stourhead

A second walk centred on the Stourhead
Estate in Wiltshire. The ramble passes through
enormously varied scenery including parkland,
grazed and arable farmland, beechwood and a
sunken green lane which used to be the old
coach road.

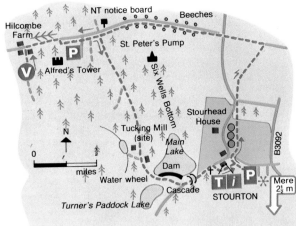

Car park: Stourhead (NT) main car park, 3m NW of
Mere. Turn off A303 to Mere, then B3092 to
Stourton village and Stourhead. Grid ref: ST 779 340.

Stourhead, the NT's most visited property (and one of its largest), is the basis for this 6¼m walk that passes through many different landscapes and takes in a fine viewpoint at the halfway stage. Some of the woodland tracks are rough in places and muddy after wet weather.

From the NT main car park at Stourhead, take the exit to Stourhead House. Do not go through the main gate to the house but enter the old turnstile to the right of it and follow the narrow made-up path. The Spanish chestnut trees on your left are probably more than 400 years old. The path continues through a kissing gate into the parkland in front of Stourhead House. At the point where the made-up path ends, bear left and make for a small gate ahead of you. Once through this cross the road and climb over the stile immediately opposite. At this point the line of the path is not clear on the ground. Do not turn left or right but, with your back to the stile, go straight ahead (roughly north) until, as the ground begins to slope down, you see three vertical poles close together. Make for these poles which are at the corner of the field on your right. Cut across the corner by unhooking and replacing two small sections of wire in the fence: *take great care* to use the insulating handles since the wire may be electrified.

Once in the field beyond, turn right and walk on with a mixed plain and barbed-wire fence on your right. At the field boundary climb over another stile and down a bank into a sunken lane. This lane is part of the old Coach Road that most recently (up to the nineteenth century) carried coaches from Salisbury to the West Country.

Turn left and follow the old Coach Road, which in May is a riot of colour with bluebells, red campion and cow parsley all thrusting their colourful blooms upwards. The attractive lane eventually gives way to a metalled road with a signpost indicating Alfred's Tower straight ahead. This minor road is at first very open with hardly a tree to be seen. As trees begin to line the way the verge on the left-hand side widens and offers a much better alternative to the road itself. Soon you are walking along an avenue of fine beech trees with the possibility of seeing bramblings in

◁ *Looking west from the chestnut-lined drive to Stourhead*

67

wintertime. Keep looking to the left and shortly a valley, Six Wells Bottom, comes into view. The obelisk is known as St Peter's Pump (NT) and is the site of the first springs of the River Stour, which soon flows out of Wiltshire to run through the length of Dorset and out to the sea at Christchurch.

Walk on through the beech trees parallel to the road and eventually you arrive at the corner of a conifer plantation on the left; continue between the plantation and the road, looking out for the NT notice board on your right. (Note this point – it marks a turn on the way back.) Very shortly you are in a clearing to the NT car park and then a long, wide green sward

△ △ *Recently-felled areas south from Alfred's Tower*
△ *Logs ready for transportation; new plantings replace them*
◁ *Despite its name, the Tower dates from George III's time*

sweeping up to Alfred's Tower (NT).

The inscription on the tablet at Alfred's Tower would appear to support the popular view that the tower marks the spot where Alfred rallied his troops against the Danish invaders in AD 879. The first lines of the inscription are: 'Alfred the Great AD 879 on this Summit erected his Standard against the Danish Invaders'. More precisely, it is recorded that the tower project dates from 1762 and it was in fact built to mark peace with France and the succession of George III in 1760. The tower is 160f high and (did you notice?) has only three sides.

As you inspect the tower you may be disappointed

that, despite the height above sea level (850f), there are no extensive views because of the surrounding trees. If so, a short ½m extension to the walk provides the answer. Go through a gap in the hedge by the tower, on the right as you approach it, to a road where you turn left. The road goes fairly steeply downhill to a track and, if the visibility is good, you should have an extensive view over Somerset.

Retrace your steps uphill, back to the tower. Make your way down the green sward, through the car park and along the clear track almost back to the NT notice board mentioned above. At this point turn right and there are two tracks in front of you. Go down the left-hand track, past the NT sign requesting that dogs should be kept on leads to protect the deer. Sadly, many deer have been cruelly mauled by dogs in the past and some have had to be put down.

This part of the walk is downhill through wood-land; there are large clearings in places but new plantings will eventually cover these. Keep to the

clearly defined track and eventually the route levels out and leads on to more open country. As you walk by a steep slope called Tucking Mill Hanging to the left, the site of Tucking Mill and a lake are on your right. Soon you are walking below the dam of the main lake in Stourhead Gardens, with the man-made cascade dropping into Turner's Paddock Lake on your right. On the bank of the lake revolves a large waterwheel that used to pump a water supply to the reservoir for Stourhead House: the wheel is now a showpiece.

Carry on to the metalled road and turn left to go under a rocky arched bridge. This carries a path from the Stourhead Gardens entrance to the Temple of Apollo – one of the classically-styled buildings which are a feature of Stourhead Gardens. The road leads to Stourton village. Go right, through the courtyard of the Spread Eagle (unless you are thirsty!) to the NT Shop and – in the season – light refreshments in the village hall. From the lower car park it is a short uphill walk back to the main car park.

◁ *A man-made waterfall cascades into Turner's Paddock Lake near the walk's end*
▷ *Stourhead's beech woods attract bramblings, winter visitors fond of beech mast (nuts)*
▽ *The arched bridge bears a path in Stourhead's jardin anglais*

Corfe & Grange Arch

The castle ruins at Corfe, and the strange folly of Grange Arch standing high above Creech village, are included in this beautiful walk through the Isle of Purbeck, west of Poole Harbour. On a sunny day walkers enjoy fine coastal views, wildflowers, birds and butterflies.

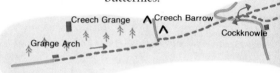

Creech Grange ∧Creech Barrow
∧
Grange Arch   Cockknowle

The towering ruins of Corfe Castle are the focal point for a vast estate of over 7,000a given to the NT by the late Mr Ralph Bankes in 1982. The castle is gaunt, stark and strangely beautiful. Creech Grange Arch, often referred to as Bond's Folly, is about 3m west of the castle. The 6½m route is along clear, well-defined paths and although there are some gradients – as one expects in hill country – the rewarding panoramic views from the tops are magnificent. The walk can be shortened to 4½m by omitting Grange Arch. After a wet spell the outward section along the side of Knowle Hill may be muddy, but in summer the tracks are normally quite dry. There are numerous gates, some with stiles adjacent, and not all are mentioned in the text. It is of course essential to ensure that gates are fastened as found since cattle may stray across the hills. Some gates have a chain and ring which drops over a peg or nail in addition to the upright iron catch.

From the car park, return along West Street to the Square and then towards the castle. Turn left and Corfe Castle entrance is on the right. Long before William invaded these islands the Saxons had a fortress at 'Corfe Gate', the gap in the hills where the ruins now stand. The murder of Edward the Martyr and long after, the defence of the castle by Lady Bankes, are fascinating episodes in the history of Corfe, which can be read in the guide books available locally.

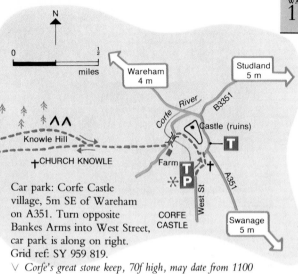

N

0 _____ ½
miles

Wareham
4 m

Studland
5 m

Corfe River

B3351

Castle (ruins)

T

Knowle Hill

+ CHURCH KNOWLE

Farm

T P

+

A351

Car park: Corfe Castle
village, 5m SE of Wareham
on A351. Turn opposite
Bankes Arms into West Street,
car park is along on right.
Grid ref: SY 959 819.

West St

CORFE
CASTLE

Swanage
5 m

∨ *Corfe's great stone keep, 70f high, may date from 1100*

Leave the castle by turning right and after only a few yards turn right along a waymarked footpath which goes round the south side of the ruins, with the little Corfe River left, to a road. Turn left at the road, cross a bridge, and continue for 30y to a gate on the right, opposite Vineyard Farm. Take the wide uphill track on the left that bends to the right. The track rises gradually to a gate by some trees. There is now a hedge on the left and this continues in one form or another for about 1m. In summertime flowers adorn hedgerow and hillside; watch out for the stinking iris which, in spite of its name, has blue flowers in July and bright orange-coloured seedheads throughout the winter. The teasel also thrives here, and although its dry deadheads stand out conspicuously in winter it is often passed unnoticed in summer since it frequently stands side by side with the dense yellow spikes of tall mullein. On the hillside (muddy in wet weather) watch out for delicate pink centaury and yellow agrimony.

At a fork do not take the main track to the right, which heads steeply uphill to a gate, but instead keep left along the hedge to a gate ahead. Soon after this you see the church at Church Knowle down the hill left, with the village mostly hidden in the trees behind it. Soon after passing a stile on the left keep a little to the right, away from the main path, and go up to a stile in a fence on the side of the hill. Pass over – or under – this

▷ *Church Knowle's church, seen on the outward section*
▽ *The track and hedge along the south of Knowle Hill*

stile and then straight ahead along a narrow path, which eventually twists round to rejoin the main path.

When you reach poles carrying a power cable, where there is also the roof of a house seen below and another house ahead (Cocknowle), keep uphill to the right. Soon you are walking beside a fence, beyond which is a minor traffic road. Follow the path until it joins the road at a gate.

The ramble can be shortened here by 2m by taking the steep uphill path, signposted back to Corfe Castle; you will pick up the longer route at the point mentioned below.

Those who wish to see the arch should keep ahead along the road and quite soon, where it bears right downhill, go straight on through a gate to commence the gradual climb up Ridgeway Hill. The track is wide between wire fences; after less than $\frac{1}{2}$m where the track turns right, go through a gate on the left.

The view is superb. Away to the south is the wide expanse of the sea; half-right is the Clavel Tower, standing on the cliff edge above Kimmeridge; straight ahead is Swyre Head; and away to the left is the sea again beyond the great hump of Ballard Down. Looking back you see Poole Harbour and the Wareham Channel; beyond are Poole and Bournemouth; and the coastline to the east finally merges with the sea and the haze. On a hot day in summer there are

Flowers (May-July)

Seedheads

◁ *The stinking iris, also
called the gladdon, thrives on
the chalky soil of the
Purbecks*

numerous butterflies, especially marbled whites which
crowd together on one thistle flower. A flash of light
swooping up and down in the sun usually means a
green woodpecker; they sometimes rise and dip like
this several times before flying away into the valley.

Through the gate, keep going in the same westerly
direction along a grassy track by the side of a hedge on
the right. The summit of Creech Barrow is on the
right, less than ½m away. There is one more gate before
you arrive at Grange Arch, where from the track the
Isle of Portland can be seen on a clear day like a low
cloud on the horizon. Far below through the clearing is
a house, Creech Grange.

The arch was built about 1740 by Denis Bond of the
Grange. Apparently he wished for an 'imposing
entrance' to his dwelling. There is no road through it,
of course, and today it is known as Bond's Folly.

△ △ *The Dorset coastline, from Ridgeway Hill near the Arch*
△ *Dennis Bond's folly – it was to be the entrance to his house*

Return by the same route to the traffic road and the gate where the shorter 4½m walk went uphill. Now you also go up the steep path straight ahead, signposted *Corfe Castle*. As the hill starts to level out there are other crossing paths, not too distinct on the ground, which gives this spot the name of Six Ways Cross. Keep eastwards and a little right of the main path there is a large flat stone with blue and yellow waymarks on it to indicate the bridleways and footpaths.

Keep straight on, along the crest of Knowle Hill. On a clear day the white chalk of the Needles headland stands out clearly. More gates-plus-stiles are encountered; press on eastwards until, soon after passing tumuli (small barrows or hillocks) on the left, the track swings to the right and goes downhill to join the outward route. Follow this back to the bridge, Corfe Castle, and the comforts of Corfe Castle village.

Golden Cap

The NT's Golden Cap Estate, nearly 2,000a on
the south coast, east of Lyme Regis, provides
the walker with hillsides, farmland, woods,
cliffs, undercliffs and beach. There is an
abundance of wildlife, and glorious views of
hill, coast and sea make the occasional steep
ascent well worthwhile.

Between Charmouth and Eypemouth sits the estate of
Golden Cap, a wonderland for the walker with 15m of
footpaths, 6m of which are on the South-West
Peninsula long-distance path. The very names in the
estate tempt one to explore this unique property: Black
Venn, Cain's Folly, Doghouse Hill, The Saddle and
Golden Cap itself, at 618f the highest cliff in the south
of England. Much of this coast has been purchased
with Enterprise Neptune funds, the NT scheme which
has probably surpassed all its earlier dreams. The walk
described here is a moderate ramble of 7½m. There are
some gradients, such as the steepish climb to Golden
Cap and the return uphill from St Gabriel's, but these
can be taken leisurely. The quality of the views and

Car park: Langdon Hill
(NT) just S off A35,
1m W of Chideock.
Grid ref: SY 412 932.
Alternative car park and
start at Stonebarrow Hill,
1½m E of Charmouth;
turn right off A35 into
Stonebarrow Lane.
Grid ref: SY 412 932.

WESTHAY

Coast Path

Stonebarrow Hill

Ridge Water

English Channel

landscape means you should allow at least four hours actual walking time. Most of the estate is actively farmed so please be particularly careful to observe the country code.

As you approach Langdon Hill car park the NT map board is near a gate on the left and a path through woods leads due south. (There is also a board and gate on the opposite side not connected with this walk.) After you have parked it is wise to return to the NT map, examine your own maps and get your bearings. Then take the track south through the woods. It goes slightly down at first, then starts to rise, and after ¼m you bear left along a little path signposted *Golden Cap*. This descends and soon joins the long-distance Coast Path (South-West Peninsula path), where you turn right. Follow the clear route over a bar-stile, uphill to another with a signpost, and beyond this is the open top of Golden Cap.

Follow the made-up path to a trig-point, where if weather permits the views are superb. Turn to the right and just beyond a memorial to Lord Antrim, who was NT chairman from 1966 until his death in 1977, go downhill to a platform-stile and head for the ruins of St Gabriel's Church, visible to the right. This

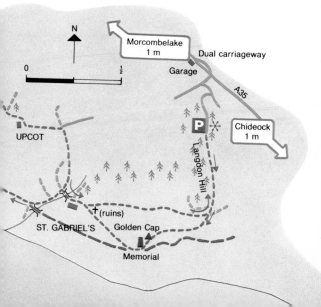

◁ Hedgerow conservation at Golden Cap supports many small birds such as the yellowhammer, one of the buntings. It feeds on the ground, sings from low trees or bushes (or telephone wires), and nests low down in thick cover

▽ The stemless (dwarf) thistle favours chalky grassland. A perennial with no stem or a very short one, its flowers are seen from July to September

◁ *Walking down from the Golden Cap trig point towards ruined St Gabriel's Church*
▽ *The route joins the coastal path, heading west towards West Hay*

church was at one time a chapel of Whitchurch Canonicorum. The date of the building is unknown, except for the south doorway which is fourteenth-century; the nave may date from this time as well. The building material is local rubble and flint. There is a legend attached to the church, related in the NT Golden Cap Estate leaflet.

From the ruins make for a large farmhouse and pass between this and the NT board, to reach a gate signposted *Coast Path*. Follow the sign, pass St Gabriel's cottage and through two gates close together, then keep by the left-hand hedge to a signpost which can be seen ahead.

Follow the Coast Path, with the sea left, across several fields and over bar-stiles. At one point you cross a small bridge over a stream; on the other side, the path is straight on to a signpost *Stonebarrow*.

As you stroll along, note that the fields have not been changed into massive prairies to suit modern farming. The NT has ensured that hedges remain and in these one may see and hear both yellowhammer and wren. On the hills and in the fields the wildflowers grow in abundance: mullein, agrimony, spear and stemless thistles are all there to delight the eye as you observe the changes from season to season.

△ *The commanding view from the summit of Golden Cap, looking westwards across the estate to Lyme Regis*
▽ *Another view of Lyme Bay, with dramatic sunlight shadowing waves in the English Channel*

Continue along the coast to the next signpost to *West Hay* and *Stonebarrow*. Turn right away from the Coast Path and make for a gate immediately to the right of a large white house (West Hay). Go through the gate, then on to another, and just beyond this turn left along a path signposted *NT Information Centre* and

Stonebarrow Car Park (the alternative start for this walk). The path is uphill and a left fork leads on to the access road across Stonebarrow Hill. Turn right for the NT Shop and then straight on to a junction of paths. In the right-hand corner go through a gate on to a bridleway signposted *St Gabriel's*.

The path is clear and there are bridleway signposts down to Upcot Farm. Bear right with the track and against the wall of a barn look straight ahead for a footpath signpost pointing left with a yellow waymark arrow. Follow this for about 300y, then turn right at another NT board indicating St Gabriel's. This leads back to the large farmhouse seen earlier. Turn left and at the chapel take a little path between it and a hedge which leads to a bridleway sign.

Keep on this track with Golden Cap away to the right. At another sign, turn right, follow the field uphill and round by a hedge, ignoring a bar-stile right, then to a gate where ahead is a view of the coastline eastwards. Turn half-right across a field to a signpost by a hedge, passed on the outward route. Turn left to a gate and from here retrace your steps back to Langdon Hill and the car park.

△ *Looking back at Golden Cap from the same viewpoint as in the photograph opposite*
▷ *The fields and hedges of the estate, seen on the return section to St Gabriel's*

Woodland Management

If you find yourself in a wood of leggy deciduous trees, all of the same age with the occasional dead 'stool' among them, you are probably standing in a once-vital part of self-sufficient rural life.

Since before the medieval period, wood was grown extensively under a system known as 'coppicing'. This was the periodic harvesting of numerous shoots or poles growing from the 'stools' (stumps) of the trees. The poles were cut off just above ground level and new shoots allowed to grow for another 15 to 25 years. Trees which have been coppiced have an unmistakable swollen base with two or more slender main trunks, still visible even in woods which have not been cut for over a century.

Coppices were also established beneath larger trees grown for timber; this was known as 'coppice-with-standards'. Several crops could be taken from the coppice while the timber trees were growing to the required height. Small timbers were used for furniture, roof woodwork and farm implements such as cart shafts and ploughs. Large timber trees were used for building houses and churches.

▽ *The coppicing method provides a variety of timber sizes from one root system. The new growths from the base are called adventitious shoots. The resulting thicket of slender trunks is called a coppice or copse*

Traditional farming communities also 'pollarded' trees, cutting them every 10 to 20 years at head height so that new shoots could grow without interference from grazing animals. The trees provided shade and shelter as well as many of the same products as coppice. Pollarded trees are also found occasionally in woods where they were used as boundary markers.

Every kind of tree was used according to its special properties. Elm, which did not split easily, was used for making wheels, while its water-resistant properties came in useful for waterwheels and coffins! Ash, an elastic wood, went for making tool handles. Oak was often grown in such a way to form natural bends or 'knees' as required by shipwrights. In the traditional woodland management system nothing was wasted: small coppiced wood was used to make brushes and thatching pins, and twigs and hedge-trimmings were 'faggoted up' into bundles and used as firewood.

In the mid-1880s some of the main uses of coppice products began to decline as coke and coal replaced charcoal as a fuel for smelting. Chemical substitutes replaced oak tan-bark in the making of leather, and general agricultural decline also meant fewer sheep hurdles and other farm implements were needed. As a result, large areas of coppice and pollard became unprofitable and were abandoned.

▷ *Results of pollarding, another pruning technique, are often seen in urban avenues where the trees provide summer shade without full branch growth*
▽ *In pollarding, growths are trimmed back to the trunk at head height*

White Sheet Hill

A third walk starting from the NT's
Stourhead Estate near Mere, Wiltshire. The
landscape is dominated by an impressive ridge
of chalk, culminating in White Sheet Hill with
its magnificent views. The open, airy nature of
the walk gives a wonderful feeling of freedom.

This 7½m walk runs south-east of Stourhead to Zeals
Knoll and Mere Castle, then north to White Sheet Hill
– an impressive chalk mound 783f high and bearing the
remnants of an iron-age hill fort and neolithic camp.
The open, exposed landscape of undulating chalk
grassland gives a marvellous sensation of freedom and
release. Indeed, such are the views on a favourable day
that this is a walk to be lingered over; on the other hand
it is unsuitable for wet, windy or very hot weather
since there are two substantial ascents and little shelter
along the route. (Walks 7 and 9 are also based at
Stourhead.)

From the Stourhead main car park leave by the
vehicle exit and turn right to pass Stourton House (not
NT but noted for its dried flowers) on the right and a
row of cottages on the left. Carry on to the B3092
road. Cross with care in the direction of a *No through
road* sign at the start of a narrow metalled road. Take
this minor road and in front of you will see your main
objective – White Sheet Hill.

The metalled section gives way to an unmade road
leading to the buildings of Search Farm. At the farm
buildings turn right and bear right along the track.
Shortly you are confronted by two gates, one single
and one double. Take the stile by the single gate and
keep near to the mixed fence and hedge on your right.
In summer watch out for small tortoiseshell butterflies
along this stretch of path. Still following the fence and
hedge, ahead of you on the right is a flattened cone-
shaped hill known as Zeals Knoll. Go through a
bridleway gate and follow the mixed fence and hedge,
which is now on your left.

As you walk south-east past Zeals Knoll, the north

86

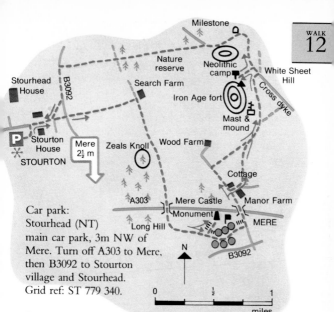

side of Long Hill and Mere Castle come into view, and
shortly afterwards a bridge over the Mere bypass
(A303). As you near the bridge, the path turns right
and almost immediately left and once again you will
find the mixed fence and hedge on the left. Cross the
substantial farm and bridleway bridge over the A303
and make for a stile on your left. Negotiate the stile and
head up the hill past an electricity post on your left.
This section, Long Hill, is a rather steep climb of 1 in 4
or more, but do not be tempted by traces of more level
tracks to the left and right.

Soon the line of the path is much clearer as it
becomes a ridge walk with views on both sides.
Continue through a kissing gate and along a stretch of
path with a thick hedge on your right-hand side – one
of the few sheltered spots on the walk. The flagpole on
the top of Mere Castle is straight ahead. Go through a
bridle gate and take a few steps to the right down on to
a well-kept grass path around the side of Mere Castle
Hill. From this path there are views south of Mere
Church and town, also Shaftesbury, Duncliffe Hill and
Bulbarrow Hill, and seats on which to rest while
consulting the maps and taking in the scene.

For an even better view of the surroundings there is a short detour, as follows. Go back to the last bridle gate and take the right-hand path which leads to brick and concrete steps; these soon bring you to the top of Mere Castle Hill. In addition to fine views in all directions, there is a memorial to the fallen of the 43rd Wessex Division in the Second World War. This is a replica of the original memorial erected on Hill 112, near Caen in Normandy – the scene of the Division's first big battle after the June 1944 invasion.

Back at the wide grass path around Mere Castle Hill, continue under trees to the top of a flight of brick and concrete steps. This is followed by a short length of path leading to another flight of steps and then a metalled road. Turn left on to the road and go across the bridge, northwards back over the A303.

Just after the approach roads to Manor Farm, turn right by a cottage. At this right turn you have to cross a cattle grid, so take great care. If members of your party find this impossible there is an alternative, but not so attractive, route as follows. Carry on along the road until you come to the entrance to Wood Farm, then

turn right on to a rather uninviting concrete road which eventually becomes a chalk track as it rises steeply. This track runs into another track coming from the right, at a point where the ridge ahead narrows between barbed-wire fences. You are now back on the main route (see below).

For those able to negotiate the cattle grid, walk along the made-up road leading away from the grid and, where it bears right, take a rough track to the left. Follow the fence on your left around a sharp left-hand bend to a gate. Through the gate, follow a clear chalky track. Keep climbing steadily; if you start going down you are on the wrong track! *Keep well clear* of the firing range as instructed by the warning notices on this stretch of the walk. At the end of the steepest part the path is less distinct but continues to follow the ridge gently upwards. There are extensive views to both sides and soon you can see the south-eastern face of the White Sheet hill fort and a radio mast. Stick to the track along the ridge. A clear track comes in from the left; this is where the walkers unable to cross the cattle grid rejoin the main route.

Small tortoiseshell

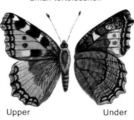

Upper · Under

Meadow brown

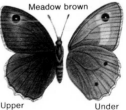

Upper · Under

△ *Two butterflies of hedgerow and rough grassland*
◁ *Their ideal habitat, with Zeals Knoll in the background*

The open space on the ridge begins to narrow between two barbed-wire fences. Follow the left-hand fence and, as it bears to the left, go through a gate and make for the mast which is surrounded by an earth mound. The earthworks of the hill fort – known as White Sheet Castle – are clearly visible on your left.

At the point where a gate on the left leads through the earth mound around the mast, turn sharp right to find yourself facing a vast expanse of downlands; this is the extreme western edge of the Wiltshire chalk downs. In the surrounding countryside can be found, in their seasons, flowers such as early purple orchids, glaucous sedge, cowslip, pyramidal orchid, devil's bit scabious, betony, harebell and horseshoe vetch. On a sunny day the marbled white, chalkhill blue and meadow brown butterflies flit from bloom to bloom.

Walk on to a gate leading to a rough track. Turn left on to the track. You are now on a very ancient road, the Coach Road, described more fully in walk 9 which also covers a section of it. Continue along this track, passing a cross-dyke which runs downhill on both sides. Shortly after this point there is a stile on your left; go over it to take in the magnificent views and to read the NT display board giving details of the White Sheet Down site. From this point you can see Stourhead House, Alfred's Tower (walk 9), Blackmoor Vale, Duncliffe Hill and Bulbarrow Hill,

◁▽ *From the steep path aiming eastwards to Mere Castle and village there are fine views of the surrounding Wiltshire countryside*

▽ *The far north-eastern section of the walk runs alongside a reserve of the Wiltshire Trust for Nature Conservation*

△ *Mere Church and town, seen from Mere Castle Hill. Mere is approximately at the halfway point of this walk and provides shelter and refreshments; the rest of the route, particularly up to White Sheet Hill, is exposed and in doubtful weather walkers should be prepared*

and you will almost certainly hear the sound of skylarks pouring out their 'full heart'.

After absorbing the views, retrace your steps from the display board to the stile and turn left on the road. Follow the road, which soon starts descending, and shortly after passing a stile on your left look out for an old milestone on the right. It bears the inscription: *XXIII Miles from Sarum 1750*. Sarum is, of course, the old name for Salisbury.

After the milestone the track runs along the boundary of a nature reserve (not open to the public) managed by the Wiltshire Trust for Nature Conservation. Where the main track starts to run under trees there is another track on the left; take this latter path which bears round to the right and heads for a clump of trees on rising ground. Walk on to and through the clump of trees and down the track known as the Drove, noting the new trees planted on either side, to join the B3092. Cross the road carefully and walk on the right-hand side (to face oncoming traffic) for a few hundred yards. At the point where the road bears left,

almost exactly opposite a *Stourton and Stourhead* road sign, leave the road and take a metalled path to the right. At the end of the path turn right into the road, and you are soon back at the car park. If you have enough puff left, Stourhead House and the exotic landscaped gardens provide a beautiful, shady contrast to the open and airy White Sheet Hill.

△ *A stile near the ancient milestone, on the way down White Sheet Hill*
◁ *Heading west on the return leg of the walk towards Stourhead, the open nature of this walk is abundantly clear. The clump of trees provides shelter not only for windblown walkers but also for wildlife – including pigeons and other crop-raiders*
▽ *More sheltering trees near the Drove trackway and B3092 road, with less than a mile to Stourhead House and the end of the walk at Stourton car park*

Leigh Woods & Avon

Leigh Woods, on the left (west) bank of the River Avon, are the base for this walk of contrasts. The route visits Stokeleigh iron-age fort, passes through seminatural forest to Abbots Leigh and Ham Green, and returns through spectacular scenery along the banks and gorge of the Avon.

Leigh Woods, 160a of mixed seminatural wood, is the NT site facing Clifton Downs on the opposite bank of the Avon. This 9m walk starts with woodland, opens out into farmed country and finishes by following the Avon upstream back to the Avon Gorge and Clifton Suspension Bridge.

Before you set off on the walk, if time permits visit the Camera Obscura on the top of the cliff, overlooking the bridge and Avon Gorge. Even if the weather is

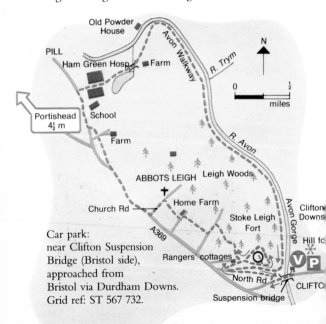

not clear enough to view through the Obscura, this is an excellent viewpoint over the river to Leigh Woods and Dundry Hill. Behind the camera tower you can see the remains of an iron-age hill fort.

Walk across the Clifton Suspension Bridge, a marvel of engineering completed by Isambard Kingdom Brunel in 1864. On the other bank immediately turn up North Road, in about $\frac{1}{2}$m reaching Leigh Woods. Enter the woodland by the main path, and by the Rangers Cottages on the left take the right fork along a grass track to Stokeleigh Hill Fort. Walk round the remains of the ramparts; if you wish, take the short cut across the plateau by turning into the next left fork and so reaching the North Access. Alternatively, continue ahead round the perimeter to reach the cliff opposite the Clifton Observatory, then turn acutely left to the North Access.

Turn left again and return to the Rangers Cottages. On reaching the clearing turn right, and 30y in front of the cottages go right again, then across a junction of paths and turn left. Continue across a path to a wall, duck under the wooden bar, and take the left fork. Follow this path through the trees by the edge of the wood for $\frac{1}{4}$m to the road. Turn left and in about 200y turn right, through the wooden gate beside the farm gate, and head straight across two fields to Home Farm. Abbots Leigh Church can now be seen in the distance beyond the farm.

△ *Brunel's engineering masterpiece, the Clifton Suspension Bridge, spans the Avon Gorge at the start of the walk*

Just before the cattle grid turn right into the
farmyard, keeping right of the timber outhouse and
left of the stone outbuildings. Close to the buildings,
go forward to a wooden gate. Through this walk on
straight towards the church, slightly left down the field
valley and ahead to the wooden stile. Climb the stile
and head for the right-hand corner of the building
which abuts the recreation ground. Cross the recreation field to arrive at Abbots Leigh Church, which
is well worth a visit. There is a memorial in the chancel
commemorating the help given by Sir George Norton
of Leigh Court to Charles II when the king escaped to
France after the battle of Worcester. At the east end of
the south aisle there is also a Norton family monu-
ment, with a canopy in the Elizabethan style. From the
front of the church there is a good view of Portishead
and the Bristol Channel.

As you come out of the church, turn right and arrive
at the end of Church Road; opposite is the George Inn
which has an impressive collection of equestrian
trappings and farm bygones. Pass the front of the inn
(unless it is refreshment time) along the raised pathway. After Harris Lane, at the bottom of the hill by the
corner, cross the road and walk through the lay-by.

◁ *One of the beautiful tree-lined tracks in Leigh Woods, between Stokeleigh Fort and Home Farm*
△ *Pastoral tranquillity at Abbots Leigh, only 3m from Bristol city centre*
▷ *Abbots Leigh Church, where there is a memorial to the help given to Charles II by Sir George Norton. The house where the king sheltered, deep in Leigh Woods, has now disappeared*

Great care is needed here since this is a main 'feeder' road from the motorway to Bristol. The footpath is again raised, first beside a stone wall and then, just past the entrance to Leigh Court Hospital (on the site of the former Leigh Court), it has a hedge on its left.

When the footpath joins the road again at Blackmoor Road, take the stile into the field where there are usually horses grazing. Cross to the next stile in the middle of the fence opposite. After a further stile, go across a farm track where you have to open (and close) a field gate. Through the gate, turn left across the field directly towards the school buildings. There is now another stile and the footpath bears left round the school playing fields. At the road which leads into Pill, turn right to pass the school and, on the left, the Anchor Inn.

Just after the Anchor turn right, down the road towards Ham Green Hospital. On reaching the roundabout with the various hospital signposts and directions, continue .straight on down the Avon walkway. Shortly afterwards an enlarged Georgian building appears on the left – the administrative offices

◁ *Leigh Woods support two species of whitebeam (*Sorbus) *found nowhere else*
▽ *An Avonside mooring bollard, testament to Bristol's former importance as a port*
▽ ▽ *Low tide on the Avon*

of the hospital. This was formerly the home of Dr Richard Bright (1789–1858), who identified and treated Bright's disease (an inflammation of the kidneys) and who was also an amateur geologist.

Go down the hill, crossing the controlled outlet at the bottom of the lake formed by a nearby spring. Continue straight ahead, turning half-right just before the farmhouse to follow the notice *Cycle bag* – the path by the Avon also being an official cyclist's route. Go through the gates, over the stile and across the well-defined footpath to the banks of the River Avon.

Immediately across the river is the old building where vessels had to discharge their gunpowder before proceeding up the river to Bristol Docks. Downstream is the vast M5 Avonmouth bridge. Turn right and after about 120y note the first of many substantial bollards formerly used for mooring ships in the river. One is marked *Society of Merchant Venturers, Bristol*, a reminder of the importance of Bristol as a port. John Cabot sailed from here on his voyage of discovery.

Follow along the river path and, depending on the tide, various wading birds can be identified on the mudflats. About 1¼m after you join the Avon the River Trym flows into it; the junction was the site of a small Roman harbour. From here to where the path starts to climb to Leigh Woods, about 2½m, is a pleasant and relaxing riverside stroll.

Soon the massive limestone cliffs of the Avon Gorge, rising to over 300f, can be seen across the river. The vertical faces are noted for their rare flora and many rock climbs. Just before reaching Bristol Suspension Bridge, opposite traffic lights on the Portway Road on the other side of the river, turn right over a stile and up into Nightingale Valley through Leigh Woods. These woods are the remnants of seminatural forest with oak, ash, witch elm, small leaved lime and two species of whitebeam (*Sorbus*) that occur nowhere else in the world. The NT co-operates with Nature Conservancy to maintain Leigh Woods as a national nature reserve. Although the path starts steeply it becomes easier, rising to the top of the valley and returning to the starting point by the NT sign. As you return over the suspension bridge the evening sun shines on the limestone cliffs, with the river flowing peacefully 250f below.

Badbury & Kingston

A fairly long walk starting at the vast iron-age
hill fort of Badbury Rings, an area steeped in
Romano-British history, and around the
perimeter of the great park of Kingston Lacy
near Wimborne Minster, Dorset. The
countryside scenery is very satisfying with
wide views across undulating fields
and woodland.

Badbury Rings is a huge iron-age hill fort at least two
thousand years old. The 'Rings' are three concentric
oval-shaped ditches and ramparts. The walk also skirts
Kingston Lacy House and Park, NT-owned but with
neither house nor park open to the public as yet. At the
halfway point the ramble passes through the village of
Pamphill where the inn provides refreshments. The
full route is about $9\frac{1}{2}$m long, though two shorter
versions of 3m and $5\frac{1}{2}$m are described. A trip around
the perimeter of the fort adds another 1m. Wear the
usual stout footwear because there are several stony
farm roads to negotiate.

From the car park make for the track that leads off
the main road, so that the Rings are on the right and a
fence boundary of a point-to-point course is immediately left. There are wide views to the north, with
Cranborne Chase on the skyline and the prominent
beech-clump of Win Green Hill.

The ancient hill fort was probably completed in its
present form about 600–500 BC, but as a human
settlement it may well go back 5,000 years. The
Romans are believed to have landed at Poole Harbour
in AD 43–44, and the legions marched northwards
under Vespasian. The tribal fort of Badbury was easily
and quickly conquered. During the subsequent occu-
pation the Romans set up what was presumably a civil
station called Vindocladia, signs of which are still
visible. Whether or not Badbury is also where the
legendary King Arthur defeated the Saxons at Mons
Badonicus in about AD 500, we may never know; but
while exploring the Rings it is nice to think so.

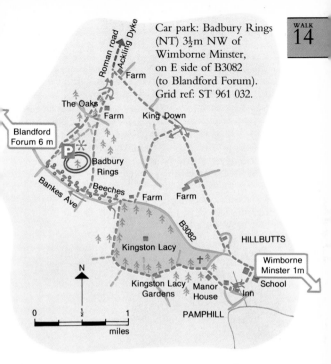

Car park: Badbury Rings
(NT) 3½m NW of
Wimborne Minster,
on E side of B3082
(to Blandford Forum).
Grid ref: ST 961 032.

For many years the fort had been neglected. Human
access and wheeled vehicles caused much damage, and
nature was not helpful either because the absence of
sheep allowed the scrub to spread and obscure the
grassy slopes of the ramparts. Since the NT acquired
Badbury a major restoration programme has been
carried out and the archaeological site is beginning to
take on its old glory. Remember that a walk around
the outer rampart will put nearly 1m on the total
distance.

Return to the track with the fenced point-to-point
course and head north-east, slightly downhill to a little
spinney where you go through a gate. Walk uphill
between wire fences to a wood, The Oaks. Many of
the trees are ivy-covered, giving a dark macabre effect,
and at one time it was thought that this wood must be
the abode of evil witches. Provided that witches are
not encountered, keep on the path and go straight on
over two crossing paths to arrive at a T-junction. This

is the Roman road from Old Sarum (Salisbury) to Badbury, from where it continued south-west.

At this junction you have a choice. For a short walk of about 3m total, turn right and continue along a farm road. Pass King Down Farm, beyond which there is a junction of tracks. A little to the right the public path passes between two large iron gates and then goes uphill towards a wood. In high summer the grasses are waist-high and this path is a mass of colour with blue scabious, purple knapweed and yellow wild parsnip; and in the sunshine the butterflies seem everywhere. Just beyond the trees the view is over the wooded park of Kingston Lacy, and away half-right on the skyline is the tower in Charborough Park. Continue to the main road, where you turn right and walk along the track by the beech avenue (described below) to return to the Badbury Rings car park.

Back at the T-junction, for the longer walks turn left along the old Roman way, which is now a farm road. After about ¼m it changes into a grassy track and farther on it becomes the Ackling Dyke, one of the finest Roman roads in Britain. Do not be tempted by the grassy track but instead keep on the farm road round a hairpin bend to pass a white farmhouse,

▷ *An ivy-covered tree in The Oaks wood, north of the Rings*
▽ *Looking north from the Rings towards Cranborne Chase*

Lambing Yard, on the left. The road drops gently down to a little valley, continues round a bend, and rises up again; ignore a road on the left.

At the next junction of paths there is another choice. Those who are feeling the strain can opt for the 5½m total route by turning right along a similar farm road. After ½m there is a barn on the left, beyond which is a crossing track. Keep straight on for another ½m, almost to the main road – but not quite. To the right through the trees is Lodge Farm, possibly one of the oldest buildings of its kind in Dorset, probably a very early hunting lodge for Cranbourne Chase. Immediately before the main road turn right on to a footpath and

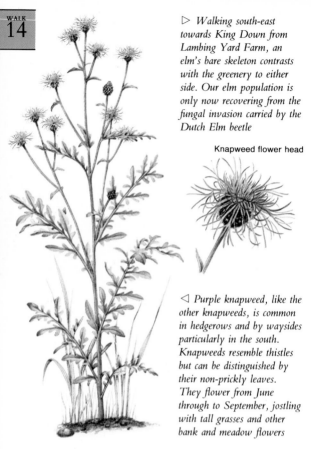

▷ Walking south-east
towards King Down from
Lambing Yard Farm, an
elm's bare skeleton contrasts
with the greenery to either
side. Our elm population is
only now recovering from the
fungal invasion carried by the
Dutch Elm beetle

Knapweed flower head

◁ Purple knapweed, like the
other knapweeds, is common
in hedgerows and by waysides
particularly in the south.
Knapweeds resemble thistles
but can be distinguished by
their non-prickly leaves.
They flower from June
through to September, jostling
with tall grasses and other
bank and meadow flowers

follow this along the beech avenue (described below)
for 1¼m to the Badbury entrance and the start.

Now only the 9½m walkers are left. At the junction
where the 5½-milers turned right you should keep
straight on, ignoring a metalled road to the left to High
Hall. Continue to another junction with cottages on
the right and, farther right, a large farm – Chilbridge
Farm. After this the surface is tarmac but it is still a
narrow lane and only farm traffic is likely.

At a point where the road turns sharp left, go
straight on to a footpath that leads uphill with a cottage
on a bank to the right. At the end of this path turn left at

a road, and immediately right for a short distance along another road. This leads to the main B3082 road at Hillbutts. Cross over and turn left for just over $\frac{1}{2}$m. After passing a thatched cottage named Lumsdens, turn right on a footpath signposted *Pamphill*. This path runs between Wimborne's Queen Elizabeth School and its playing fields.

Go over a stile, along by the side of a wire fence, and when this ends turn right down the hill. Make for a pylon, which is the turning point for overhead cables, by crossing a little stream in the valley, climbing a stile located in the right-hand corner of a field, and walking uphill over another stile. At the pylon turn left to the road at Pamphill.

The ramble continues to the right (north-west) but by turning left for a short distance you can refresh yourself at The Vine Inn. This tiny hostelry was originally built as a bakery, but has been a pub for well over a hundred years.

Rambling again, the road passes under the power cables and the village school is on the right. Cross Pamphill Green through an avenue of oaks and arrive at a crossing road where you should turn left. Before turning, however, look straight ahead for St Stephen's

△ *Cattle graze near King Down, east of Badbury Rings*

Church. This was built in 1907 in Kingston Lacy Park by the trustees of W R Bankes, who left funds for the purpose. Although known as Kingston Lacy Church it is also the parish church for Pamphill – since there is no longer a village of Kingston Lacy.

After turning left the walk along the lane is a little under ¾m, with Kingston Lacy Park on the right. After cottages there is a wrought-iron gate left, leading to the kitchen gardens of the great house – hence the name of Kingston Lacy Gardens (as opposed to the Park). Just beyond this gate the road turns sharply left but your route is straight ahead through a gate. In late winter and early spring this part of the park is white with snowdrops.

After the gate there is a wide green track around the outside of Kingston Lacy Park to the main B3082 road; as you walk, ignore all similar tracks to the left. The great house is hidden among the trees on the right. At the main road the magnificent avenue of beeches (mentioned above) commences and runs eastwards for 1½m. It was planted by W J Bankes in 1835 and legend has it that there were 365 trees on one side and 366 (for leap years) on the other; you might like to check, but

△ △ *The Vine Inn, Pamphill, was originally a bakery*
△ *Part of the track skirting south and west of Kingston Lacy*

today there are gaps here and there along the rows. By crossing the road there is a pleasant path running left parallel to the beeches and sufficiently away from the road to make the traffic less noticeable. Stroll beneath the beeches all the way back to Badbury Rings entrance and the start. (Do not try any short-cuts across to the Rings since there are no rights of way.)

Weston & Sand Bay

This seashore walk follows the line of Sand Bay, north of Weston-super-Mare. The route goes through woodland and passes an iron-age hill fort, crosses the extensive sands of the bay and circles the limestone peninsula of Sand Point for excellent views of the Bristol Channel.

In the area of Sand Bay and Sand Point there are several NT sites, and this 10m walk visits three of them: the limestone headland of Sand Point; Middle Hope and Woodspring Priory to the east (though the priory itself is not open to visitors); and the ancient flight of Monk's Steps near Kewstoke Church. As with all coastal walks you should enquire about local weather conditions and tides, and *never* take chances by wandering on to sandflats where you may be cut off by the tide.

Park by Birnbeck Pier, on the north side of Weston-super-Mare just past the Royal Pier Hotel. Walk up to Kewstoke Road, and almost immediately turn right up a rough track marked *Weston Woods and Ancient British Encampment*. The path climbs through the deciduous trees, though when you reach the stone steps on the right you might make a detour up these to view the iron-age hill fort. The principal remains are dilapidated stone-wall fortifications. More information on the fort can be obtained from the museum at Weston-super-Mare.

Return down the stone steps to the Weston Woods forest track and turn right back on to the route. In about $\frac{1}{3}$m there is a tree surrounded by benches; take the right-hand track along the bridleway. In $\frac{1}{4}$m pass the water tower where five ways meet and where the track changes to road, entering the edge of Kewstoke to become Worlebury Hill Road. Go through the spinney of trees and take the first right into Furze Road. Just before turning into Furze Road there is a view of Sand Point and beyond into Wales. Swing left along Furze Road and then right into Woodspring Avenue, which bends sharp left and right again and in

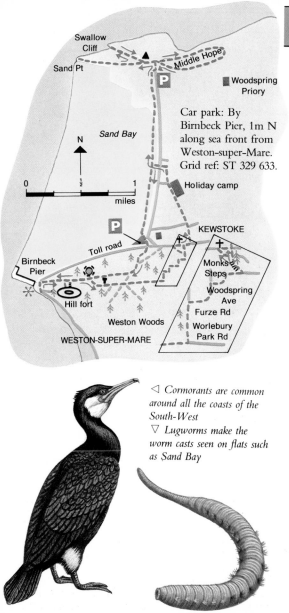

Swallow
Cliff

Sand Pt

Middle Hope

■ Woodspring
Priory

Car park: By
Birnbeck Pier, 1m N
along sea front from
Weston-super-Mare.
Grid ref: ST 329 633.

Sand Bay

N

0   ½   1
miles

Holiday camp

KEWSTOKE

Toll road

Birnbeck
Pier

Monks
Steps

Woodspring
Ave

Furze Rd

Hill fort

Worlebury
Park Rd

Weston Woods

WESTON-SUPER-MARE

◁ Cormorants are common
around all the coasts of the
South-West
▽ Lugworms make the
worm casts seen on flats such
as Sand Bay

△ One of the clearings in
Weston Woods, on the edge
of Kewstoke village
▷ △ Kewstoke Church,
near the bottom of Monk's
Steps leading to Sand Bay
▷ Monk's Steps, from
where there are views over
the Severn Estuary and
towards Bristol. Also known
as St Kew's Steps, they were
donated to the NT in 1936
by Mr H Butt. Their
origins are obscure; they
certainly date from medieval
times. Besides the steps
themselves the NT owns 2½a
of adjacent land

about 100y arrives at the top of Monk's Steps.

The Steps were used in medieval times and are now
owned and maintained by the NT. They wind down
again on to the road, into Kewstoke. To make a
recommended detour to visit Kewstoke Church, turn
left at the bottom of the Steps and at the foot of Monk's
Hill turn right. Alternatively, or after the church visit,
at the foot of Monk's Steps cross over the road and go
through a high stone stile down a very steep footpath

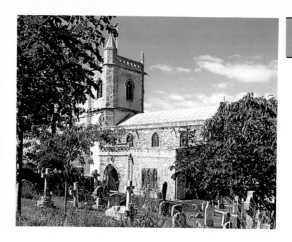

to arrive opposite the entrance to St Paul's Church, Kewstoke.

As you enter St Paul's outside porch notice the thirteenth-century lancet door and also the ancient iron-studded oak door leading into the church, set in a magnificent and well-preserved Norman archway. The stone pulpit is fifteenth-century, with elaborate carving. It is believed that many carved stone pulpits in this area were the work of a travelling band of masons.

There is an old story linking St Paul's Church to Woodspring Priory nearby to the north. In 1849, during repairs to the north wall of the nave, a casket of relics was found hidden behind a piece of carved stone. In the back of this reliquary was a carved recess that held a small wooden cup containing traces of a dark substance. It is believed to be one of the wooden cups sold by the Monks of Canterbury, who claimed the cups contained water mixed with drops of the blood of St Thomas à Becket. This cup is now held in Taunton Museum.

After the visit to the church turn left as you leave, past the Earls Crest Hotel and down a road signposted to Sand Bay. In about ¾m, where the road bends sharp left, take the footpath to the right of the corner marked *Pontins and Beach Road*. At the end of the first section of the footpath, walk across the front of the holiday camp and continue along through the stile (*Public Footpath* sign) diagonally across the field to the north-west corner. The footpath then leads to Beach Road, running parallel with the sands. Arriving at the Long John Silver public house, cross Beach Road and stroll northwards along the open sands to Sand Point.

From the beach there are excellent views: Steep Holm and Flat Holm islands; back towards Burnham Pier at Weston; and westwards to the Welsh coast. It is quite common to see cormorants and other waders, such as curlews, in this area.

As you approach Sand Point continue along the path near the sand dunes to the sea wall. Turn right at the end of the wall, immediately before the cliff, and up the steps on to a path climbing to Sand Point. On reaching the trig-point walk out along the cliff top to the end of the headland and savour the impressive views over the Bristol Channel.

On your return to the trig-point there is a narrow path leading down to a bay on the north side of the peninsula next to Swallow Cliff. At low tide it is possible to see a 'raised beach' formed half a million years ago. Volcanic lava also occurs on this side of the peninsula.

Walk eastwards from the point along the coast path and there are distant views of the Mendip Hills, with the tower of Woodspring Priory in the foreground.

Continue eastwards, past the path you climbed from the bay, out on to the north side of Middle Hope. Climb the ladder stile over the wall, continuing on the path that follows the coastline. You come to a point where access ceases, since there is no footpath across the farmland by the remains of the priory. Return instead along the south side of Middle Hope, down to Sand Bay again and southwards back along the beach past the convalescent home to the car park at the end, where steps lead up to the toll road.

Go straight across the road into Weston Woods and up a steep narrow path with signs of quarrying on the right. Climb as far as the main path through the woods, and turn right. Continue until you see five posts blocking the pathway about 100y ahead; at this point take the right-hand fork. In a short while you are back at the tree surrounded by benches. Continue down through the woods, retracing your steps to the starting point.

▽ *The Mendips on the skyline, from the north of Sand Point. From the steps up to Sand Point there are marvellous views south along Sand Bay to Weston and beyond* ▽
The steep path back into Weston Woods, on the return leg ▽ ▽

Brean Down

The bold headland of Brean Down, which is
the southern arm of Weston Bay near
Weston-super-Mare, gives commanding views
of Somerset and the Bristol Channel. The
route takes in Brean Sands and a peaceful
riverside section along the Axe.

Brean Down (NT), 2m south-west of Weston-super-
Mare town, juts into the Bristol Channel and from its
320f trig-point there are magnificent views in all
directions. The Berrow Sands to the south are a
declared site of special scientific interest on account of
their rich plant and animal life. This 10m walk takes
most of the day, even without stops to take in the
scenery and watch birds wading on the shoreline.

Park considerately at Ford Common, cross the road
and walk westwards along the track towards the
caravan park, passing through a wide wooden gate. At
the camp shop carry straight on through the iron gate
to the road. Turn left and then immediately right
across the road, along the bridleway through the sand
dunes. As you bear north along the beach, Brean
Down dominates the landscape at the end of the sands.

At low tide the ribs of an old ship can be seen rising
out of the sands. These are the remains of the

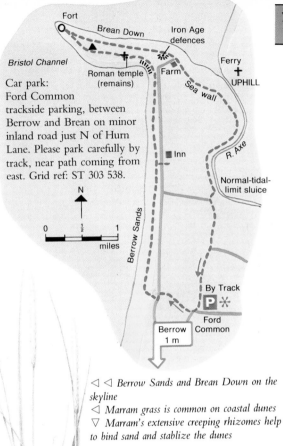

Fort

Brean Down

Iron Age defences

Bristol Channel

Ferry

UPHILL

Roman temple (remains)

Farm

Sea wall

Car park:
Ford Common
trackside parking, between
Berrow and Brean on minor
inland road just N of Hurn
Lane. Please park carefully by
track, near path coming from
east. Grid ref: ST 303 538.

R. Axe

Inn

N

0   ½   1
miles

Berrow Sands

Normal-tidal-limit sluice

By Track

P ✳

Ford Common

Berrow
1 m

◁ ◁ *Berrow Sands and Brean Down on the skyline*
◁ *Marram grass is common on coastal dunes*
▽ *Marram's extensive creeping rhizomes help to bind sand and stablize the dunes*

WALK
16

Norwegian barque *Nornen*, driven ashore by heavy seas in 1897 after losing all her sails in a storm. The sand dunes area has been declared a site of special scientific interest on account of its rich plant and animal life. Marram grass and other plant pioneers stabilize the sand so that other, less brave plants and animals can live in some sort of shelter. There should now be good views of the two islands, Steep Holm and Flat Holm, farther away to the right. These are, with Brean Down itself, limestone extensions of the Mendip Hills. Steep Holm is a bird sanctuary and a breeding place for gulls, who fly over to the mainland shore to pick at the debris of the strand line when the tide recedes.

After walking along the beach for about 2m there is a footpath through the sand dunes to the parallel road and the Brean Down Inn, to which you can detour for refreshments.

▷ *The strand line left by high tides is a nature detective's paradise. Mermaid's purses (skate or dogfish egg cases) and cuttle bones (the internal shells of cuttlefish) are two of the items donated by the sea*
▽ *The muddy tidal banks of the River Axe complement the sands of Berrow and attract a variety of seabirds*

Leave the beach 1m farther north, by the cafe, to climb the steps to Brean Down. In the sand cliff to the left of the steps bones of Arctic fox and reindeer half a million years old have been found. Arriving on top of the down, take the well-worn path to the trig-point past the Roman Temple site, identified by unevenness in the ground on the left. Near the trig-point there are signs of a Celtic field system, possibly dating from iron-age or Roman times. Continue westwards to the fort at Brean Point. The fort was built in 1867 as protection against a possible invasion by Napoleon, but was abandoned at the end of the nineteenth century when the magazine exploded. It was subsequently used in both World Wars.

Return eastwards by the military tarmac road with excellent views over Weston Bay to Birnbeck Pier, Worlebury Hill and beyond to Sand Point (walk 15). Just before the hairpin bend back to the beach road, note more remains of iron-age defences on the right. Keep in the same direction past the hairpin bend and take the footpath over the wooden stile, heading down to the farm and the River Axe ferry. This path tends to be overgrown in summer but should be on the map and is passable with care.

At the farm turn right along the sea wall to the ferry. This operates only in summer (though you do not need to take it), crossing to Uphill in Weston-super-Mare. You follow the route along the raised west bank for some 2m from Brean Farm to the sluice gate at the normal tidal limit. While walking this part it is well worth turning round occasionally to enjoy the panoramic view. Brent Knoll is in the south and, anti-clockwise, Uphill Church is on the hill over the river. Weston Bay is north and Crook Peak can be seen to the west. In addition to the views there are many different species of birds to be seen. Brean Down has been a bird sanctuary since 1912, and spring and autumn bring migratory flocks of ducks and waders to the down and sands.

Skirt the fence by the entrance to the sluice and follow the tarmac to the road ahead. Leaving the double wooden gates, turn left and walk until you reach the next road junction where you turn right with the signpost *Berrow*. In about $\frac{3}{4}$m you return to the starting point at Ford Common.

Clevedon & Cadbury

This lengthy and undulating walk connects two NT properties south-west of Bristol – the iron-age hill fort at Cadbury Camp and the manor at Clevedon Court. The route crosses the Gordano Valley, which runs between the two sites, and also takes in fine coastal views from Back Hill and Walton Down.

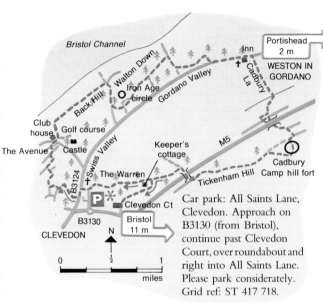

Car park: All Saints Lane, Clevedon. Approach on B3130 (from Bristol), continue past Clevedon Court, over roundabout and right into All Saints Lane. Please park considerately. Grid ref: ST 417 718.

Clevedon Court, set in 14½a of gardens, is an interesting manor house with sections built in every century since the thirteenth, though the main house is four-teenth-century. Across the Gordano Valley on Tickenham Hill is the 39½a site of Cadbury Camp, containing an iron-age hill fort. This 11m walk connects the two; the valley is split by the M5 motorway but resourceful walkers have devised a route crossing even this seemingly impassable barrier. The paths can be vague and good maps are essential.

Leave All Saints Lane by Walton Road, turning left. Looking to the right above Swiss Valley is Walton Castle (privately owned), a sham castle built in the reign of James I. In 100y turn right, up Strawberry Hill. Where the hill levels out and just past a *No Motorcycles* notice leave the metalled road by a path to the left of an upright stone post, and enter the woods. This path climbs to join a wider footpath where you turn right. The path soon narrows again, however, past a wooden post and then round the back of a house where it turns left to a road. In 20y turn right and continue to the end of this road. On reaching the end of Rippleside Road turn right and, in about 450y at Edward Road, turn right again past the pillarbox. Follow Edward Road round into Edward Road West; in 300y at The Avenue turn right and then almost immediately left, and cross over another road. You are now at the entrance to Castle Farm, Clevedon Golf Club and Walton Castle.

Walk through the entrance and up the road but beware of golfers playing across your route! On reaching the *Public Footpath* signs turn left towards the golf clubhouse. Continue over the stile and along the footpath to the top of Back Hill with views westwards over the Bristol Channel to the Welsh coast. The footpath passes between brambles by the side of the golf course and the vegetation on this narrow path provides a good habitat for butterflies, seen in profusion in the summer months.

△ *From the top of Back Hill there are fine views of the Bristol Channel, Wales, south to Devon, and north to Aust*

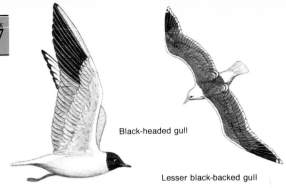

Black-headed gull

Lesser black-backed gull

Climb another stile and on a clear day you can see the Severn Suspension Bridge at Aust. The path drops down gently to a junction where you turn right towards a road. Again turn right, down the hill for about 400y. Now turn left up another path marked *No Motorcycles*. This path climbs up and contours along the southern side of Walton Down. Eventually the path reaches the top of the hill where there is an iron-age earthen circle. Follow the path north-eastwards at this level and where it forks, keep to the left and straight on into the woods. Pass through a wooden gate with a notice regarding right of way. At the end of the wood take the waymarked footpath to the right, entering a field by a stile.

Now there is a good view across the Gordano Valley to the motorway on the south side. Despite its presence, one has to marvel at the interesting engineering feature of carrying traffic at split levels. Turn left in the field and follow the wood running along the top side. This part of the walk is known by local inhabitants as Church Walk. At the far side of the field go through the gate in the corner and turn right, through the edge of the wood into the next field. Again keep along the top of the field and close to the wood. The village of Weston-in-Gordano has now come into view. Having reached the far corner of this field turn at right-angles down the fence, past the *Bristol Waterworks* tank on the other side of the fence, and leave the field by the gate. Turn left to join the road into Weston-in-Gordano.

When you arrive at the White Hart (or after leaving this inn) continue for about 200y and then turn right

◁ ▷ *Many species of gull
wheel over the waters of the
Bristol Channel, where refuse
from ships and the large
coastal towns provide them
with easy picking*
▽ *One of the paths
on the descent from Walton
Down to Weston-in-Gordano*
▽ ▽ *The church at
Weston-in-Gordano, on the
walk's northernmost section*

Common gull

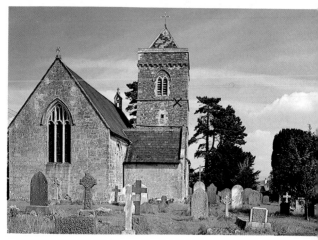

along Cadbury Lane. Carry on straight down the lane, noting the peat beds on the bottom near the right. At the foot of the lane, cross the dyke by the bridge and pass through the gate, turning immediately right by the dyke to the next gate. After going through this gate turn diagonally left, across the field, towards an oak tree. Pass through the gate immediately behind the oak. Turn left along the hedgerow and in 40y right, upwards along the edge of the field to the top. A right turn and another 40y bring you through the gate on to the road.

Turn left on the road for 150y and then take a right up the rough track to pass under the M5 motorway by Wynhol Cattery. In $\frac{1}{4}$m take a narrow footpath on the right, which tends to be overgrown but still passable in summer. This leads to a track and opposite is the NT *Cadbury Camp* notice to which a public footpath runs. Walk along this footpath, past a display board explaining the iron-age hill fort which was built around 500 BC. The structure of the ridge, Tickenham Hill, is carboniferous limestone formed 200 million

years ago. Views from the top of Tickenham Hill extend to the Mendip Hills in the south, westwards to Weston-super-Mare Bay, and north to the Bristol Channel and the coast of Wales.

After exploring the fort take the footpath to the west, returning to the track along Tickenham Hill. Leave by the stile and continue in a general westerly direction along the lane for 1m. After passing the gateways to one or two houses, take the right-hand fork where the lane divides and in a short distance cross the footbridge back over the motorway. On the other side go up the road and straight through the wide wooden gate to the inviting footpath beyond. It is worth glancing back at this point to see how the motorway cutting has reshaped the landscape. One wonders whether such 'earthworks' will receive the attention, in centuries to come, that we currently give to, say, iron-age forts.

The walk enters the cool shade of trees until the path emerges again by Keepers Cottage. You are now at Court Hill and about to pass through Norton Wood

△ The path heading south from the motorway underpass up to Cadbury Camp, on the ridge of Tickenham Hill
◁ One of the dykes in the Gordano valley, on the section between Weston-in-Gordano village and the motorway underpass

△ *Not only walkers appreciate the grassy ridge of Tickenham Hill and the views to the Mendips and Weston*
▷ *The pretty path between motorway and Keepers Cottage Keepers Cottage marks the detour point to Clevedon Court* ▽

and the Warren. For Clevedon Court and Gardens (see NT handbook for opening times) turn sharp left at Keepers Cottage and follow the main track down, round a hairpin to the right, and then on again in the same direction to arrive at the house.

Clevedon Court dates chiefly from 1320 when Sir John de Clevedon built the manor, and it is one of the few surviving houses from this period. One of the oddities contained within is a collection of Nailsea glass from the nearby factory; interesting but totally impractical are the famous glass walking sticks, rolled and marbled like sticks of seaside rock.

After visiting the house and strolling round the gardens, return to Keepers Cottage and turn left to continue the original path over the Warren. Keep left going downhill to enter the old woodland. Take the next right and then the immediate left-hand track. In about 200y pass a rock seat, and then reach the edge of the wood in a further 300y. Zig-zag down to the left, passing railings on the right, until a way between rocks appears and leads to an iron gate. Go through this, descending in the same general direction, down the steps and back to the start at All Saints Church.

Useful information

The NT owns and protects well over 500,000a in England, Wales and Northern Ireland – about one per cent of the total land area. It is perhaps best known for its great country houses with their gardens and parks, but it was not for these that the organization came into existence in 1895. At that time the countryside itself and its smaller buildings were under threat, as towns and suburbs spread and places like the Lake District began to feel the full impact of the newly-mobile population. The first property acquired by the NT was a mere $4\frac{1}{2}$a of clifftop at Dinas Oleu, near Barmouth in Gwynedd. Its first building was the historic but modest mid fourteenth-century Clergy House at Alfriston, East Sussex.

Today, the NT looks after 450m of the finest unspoilt coastline. It has 1,100 tenanted farms, and cares for one-quarter of the Lake District National Park and one-tenth of Snowdonia. There are huge tracts of NT land in the Peak District, South Wales, Dorset and Somerset, together with parts of the Malvern and Shropshire Hills and the Isle of Wight, and there are innumerable other NT properties scattered across the country.

When you are walking on NT land, look searchingly at your surroundings. Note how the woods, fields and copses are managed, how the paths are laid out and maintained, and how local features such as stiles, walls, barns and fences are looked after and renovated in keeping with the character of the countryside.

The NT's twin aims of access and conservation take time and money. The work is based on detailed management plans, often drawn up in consultation with bodies such as the Nature Conservancy Council, Countryside Commission, local county councils, and naturalists' and archaeological trusts. Walkers who gain pleasure from NT facilities can reciprocate by joining the NT – a charity that looks after large tracts of land and buildings for you, and for future generations, to enjoy for ever.

The National Trust, Central Office, 36 Queen
Anne's Gate, London SW1H 9AS;
phone 01-222 9251
Membership enquiries to: The National Trust,
Membership Department, PO Box 30, Beckenham,
Kent BR3 4TL; phone 01-650 7263
The National Trust, **Wessex Regional Office**,
Stourton, Warminster, Wiltshire BA12 6QD;
phone Bourton, Dorset (0747) 840224
Avon Wildlife Trust, 209 Redland Road, Bristol
Dorset Naturalists' Trust, 39 Christchurch Road,
Bournemouth, Dorset BH1 3NS
Somerset Trust for Nature Conservation, Fyne
Court, Broomfield, Bridgwater, Somerset
TA5 2EQ
Wiltshire Trust for Nature Conservation,
19 High Street, Devizes, Wiltshire
Ramblers' Association, 1/5 Wandsworth Road,
London SW8 2LJ; phone 01-582 6878
Ordnance Survey, Romsey Road, Maybush,
Southampton SO9 4DH

Walkers are advised to plan their outings using
current NT information for details of opening days
and times and admission fees. Two invaluable
sources are *Properties of the National Trust* and the
Properties Open booklets relating to the region in
question.

Acknowledgements

Thanks are due to the following people for devising routes and writing walk accounts and features:
C Lloyd Adams, Ken Fisher, Ernest Green, Rachael Griffiths, Priscilla Houston, Marjorie Straton, C Trent Thomas

Thanks also to the following for their help:
Glenys Blackall, Tom Burr, Sue Clark, Bill Pethybridge, Gill Raikes, Ramblers' Association, Anne Warwicker

Illustrations by Andrew Aloof, Bob Bampton, Sandra Pond, Will Giles, Michael McGuinness

Walk and locator map   Cooper West

Art work visualiser   Mike Trier

Additional photography   Alan North – page 21 – courtesy of The National Trust

The publishers are grateful to the following companies and individuals:
Blacks of Holborn for camping equipment, Nikon UK Ltd for camera equipment, Fred and Kathy Gill, Format Publishing Service, Diana Greenman and Jane Parker